U.S. Bureau of Immigration

Annual report of the Commissioner-General of Immigration to the Secretary of Commerce and Labor

U.S. Bureau of Immigration

Annual report of the Commissioner-General of Immigration to the Secretary of Commerce and Labor

ISBN/EAN: 9783741140877

Manufactured in Europe, USA, Canada, Australia, Japa

Cover: Foto ©Suzi / pixelio.de

Manufactured and distributed by brebook publishing software (www.brebook.com)

U.S. Bureau of Immigration

Annual report of the Commissioner-General of Immigration to the Secretary of Commerce and Labor

OF THE

COMMISSIONER-GENERAL OF IMMIGRATION

TO THE

SECRETARY OF COMMERCE AND LABOR

FOR THE

FISCAL YEAR ENDED JUNE 30, 1905

WASHINGTON
GOVERNMENT PRINTING OFFICE
1905

Department of Commerce and Labor

Document No. 42

BUREAU OF IMMIGRATION

2

JV
6419

ANNUAL REPORT

OF THE

COMMISSIONER-GENERAL OF IMMIGRATION.

DEPARTMENT OF COMMERCE AND LABOR,
BUREAU OF IMMIGRATION,
Washington, D. C., July 1, 1905.

SIR: In presenting the report of the Bureau of Immigration for the fiscal year ended June 30, 1905, I have the honor to urge upon your attention the significance of the figures contained in the usual tabulations furnished to show in a condensed form the most conspicuous facts in relation to alien immigration. Some analysis will be necessary to an intelligent comprehension of the import to the well-being both of alien arrivals, and, what is far more important, to the welfare of our own people, of the continuous influx in such a vast tide of peoples of the most widely varying aims and capacities. To make room for some such analysis the reports of officers of the Bureau have been omitted, only such parts thereof as seem to require mention being embodied in the text.

The experience of another year, while it has brought a gratifying confirmation of the confidence heretofore expressed in the efficiency of existing administrative measures and agencies, has also served to establish a stronger conviction of the magnitude and gravity of the problems presented by the growth of our alien population. These problems loom so largely in the prospect of our country that it may be said, without giving just cause to charge exaggeration, that all other questions of public economy, relating to things rather than to human beings, shrink into comparative insignificance.

While an endeavor has been made to condense this report by the careful omission of everything not indispensable to its completeness, with these views of the pressing importance of the subject, it has seemed inconsistent with my sense of duty as a public servant to omit such a treatment of the subject as will avoid the misconceptions, or the inadequate comprehension, resulting from a merely formal and colorless recital of what the Bureau has accomplished during the past year.

It should be borne in mind, as bearing upon the amount of work accomplished by the immigration officers, that the total of alien arrivals reported for the year, 1,026,499, does not represent all whose coming has necessitated inspection. Besides these there are many others who ultimately submit to officers proof of their citizenship, and these, although inspected, are not enumerated in the following tables. Thus, at the port of New York 126,296 passengers were examined as apparent aliens, but were admitted subsequently as citizens. It is also to

3

be noted that the above total does not include aliens landed in the United States to pass through to othr " countries.

TABLE I.—REPORT OF ALIENS (EXCLUSIVE OF ALIENS IN TRANSIT) ADMITTED INTO THE UNITED STATES, BY PORTS, DURING THE FISCAL YEARS ENDED JUNE 30, 1904 AND 1905.

Port.	1904.			1905.		
	Males.	Females.	Total.	Males.	Females.	Total.
New York, N. Y	405,097	200,922	606,019	553,084	235,135	788,219
Boston, Mass	37,327	22,951	60,278	38,460	26,647	65,107
Baltimore, Md	40,240	15,700	55,940	47,638	14,676	62,314
Philadelphia, Pa	12,194	7,273	19,467	15,224	8,600	23,824
San Francisco (including Los Angeles district and San Diego)	7,742	1,294	9,036	5,332	1,045	6,377
Bangor, Me	3		3	27		27
Brunswick, Ga	1		1	15		15
Douglas, Ariz				43	3	46
Eagle Pass, Tex	266	74	340	186	71	257
El Paso, Tex	430	51	481	704	129	833
Fernandina, Fla				3		8
Galveston, Tex	1,029	743	1,772	1,861	906	2,767
Gulfport, Miss. (including Pascagoula and Shieldsboro)	12		12	127	4	131
Honolulu, Hawaii	7,841	1,213	9,054	10,794	1,203	11,997
Jacksonville, Fla	11	6	17	13	4	17
Ketchikan, Alaska	19	1	20	4	1	5
Key West, Fla	3,788	1,480	5,268	5,597	2,491	8,088
Laredo, Tex				685	145	830
Miami and Tampa, Fla	175	108	283	274	129	403
Mobile, Ala	143	39	182	241	67	308
Naco, Ariz				209	1	210
New Bedford, Mass	2,236	1,531	3,767	1,354	844	2,198
New Orleans, La	3,576	1,370	4,946	2,842	1,158	4,000
Nogales, Ariz				78	6	84
Norfolk, Va. (including Newport News and Old Point Comfort)	408	34	442	159	6	165
Pensacola, Fla	5		5	129		129
Portland, Me	359	163	522	401	167	568
Portland, Oreg	336	19	355	38	3	41
Providence, R. I	42	15	57			
San Juan, P. R. (including Ponce)	1,267	421	1,688	1,167	427	1,594
Savannah, Ga				19		19
Seattle, Wash. (including Port Townsend and Tacoma)	2,360	180	2,540	1,541	164	1,705
Tucson, Ariz				4		4
Wilmington, Del	1		1			
Total United States	526,908	255,588	782,496	688,253	294,032	982,285
Through Canada via— Montreal (including Quebec, Point Levis, St. John, Halifax, and all border stations)	16,780	7,637	24,417	33,493	7,083	40,576
Vancouver (including Victoria)	5,412	545	5,957	3,168	470	3,638
Total Canada	22,192	8,182	30,374	36,661	7,553	44,214
Grand total	549,100	263,770	812,870	724,914	301,585	1,026,499

Next after the large increases shown for the year in the arrivals at the principal ports of entry—New York, Boston, Philadelphia, and Baltimore—the specially observable features of the foregoing table are the decreases reported for the Pacific ports and the increases at southern ports. The former may be accounted for in some measure by the war in the East. Of the latter more will be said elsewhere.

From Table I it appears that there entered at—

United States continental ports	968,694
United States insular ports	13,591
Total through United States ports	982,285
Through Canadian ports	44,214
Grand total	1,026,499

The increase over the corresponding figures for the next preceding fiscal year is 213,629, of which the continental ports of the United States report 196,940, as compared with arrivals thereat last year and the Canadian ports 13,840. As to our insular ports, there is an increase shown of 2,849, although the arrivals at Porto Rico were less by 94 than in 1904.

TABLE II.—COMPARATIVE STATEMENT SHOWING THE NUMBER OF ALIENS ADMITTED INTO THE UNITED STATES, BY COUNTRIES, DURING THE FISCAL YEARS ENDED JUNE 30, 1904 AND 1905, RESPECTIVELY, SHOWING INCREASE AND DECREASE FOR EACH COUNTRY.

Country.	1904.	1905.	Increase.	Decrease.
Austria-Hungary	177,156	275,693	98,537	....
Belgium	3,976	5,302	1,326	....
Denmark	8,525	8,970	445	....
France, including Corsica	9,406	10,168	762	....
German Empire	46,380	40,574	....	5,806
Greece	11,343	10,515	....	828
Italy, including Sicily and Sardinia	193,296	221,479	28,183	....
Netherlands	4,916	4,954	38	....
Norway	23,808	25,064	1,256	....
Portugal, including Cape Verde and Azore islands	6,715	5,028	....	1,687
Roumania	7,087	4,437	....	2,650
Russian Empire and Finland	145,141	184,897	39,756	....
Servia, Bulgaria, and Montenegro	1,325	2,043	718	....
Spain, including Canary and Balearic islands	3,996	2,600	....	1,396
Sweden	27,763	26,591	....	1,172
Switzerland	5,023	4,269	....	754
Turkey in Europe	4,344	4,542	198	....
United Kingdom:				
England	38,626	64,709	26,083	....
Ireland	36,142	52,945	16,803	....
Scotland	11,092	16,977	5,885	....
Wales	1,730	2,503	773	....
Europe, not specified	143	13	....	130
Total Europe	767,933	974,273	206,340	....
China	4,809	2,166	....	2,143
Japan	14,264	10,331	....	3,933
India	261	190	....	71
Turkey in Asia	5,235	6,157	922	....
Other Asia	2,117	5,081	2,964	....
Total Asia	26,186	23,925	....	2,261
Africa	686	757	71	....
Australia, Tasmania, and New Zealand	1,461	2,091	630	....
Philippine Islands	52	39	....	13
Pacific islands, not specified	42	36	....	6
British North America	2,837	2,168	....	669
British Honduras	109	123	14	....
Other Central America	605	1,072	467	....
Mexico	1,009	2,637	1,628	....
South America	1,667	2,576	909	....
West Indies	10,193	16,641	6,448	....
All other countries	90	161	71	....
Total	812,870	1,026,499	213,629	....
Aliens in transit	27,844	33,256	5,412	....
Total alien passengers	840,714	1,059,755	219,041	....

The increase of 213,629 shown by Table I is made up of the arrivals from four countries of Europe, Austria-Hungary sending an additional number over its quota for last year of 98,537, Russia of 39,756, Italy of 28,183, and the United Kingdom of 49,544. This encouraging increase from the last-mentioned country is somewhat offset by decreases from Germany, Switzerland, and Sweden. Notwithstanding the reported increase of 28,183 from Italy, that country may be regarded as having probably reached the high-water mark, since two years ago her contribution to our immigration was 230,622, or 9,430 in excess of the figures for the past year. The countries, therefore, which may be regarded as the chief sources of future increases in immigration are those two in Europe which have the greatest resources in population, probably, to dispense with—Russia and Austria-Hungary. With these facts in view it will be possible to calculate with reasonable certainty on the character of immigration, in its greater bulk, for some years to come—at least of European immigration.

As regards Asiatic immigration, the reported decrease in arrivals from China of about one-half of the number given in the last annual report brings the total down to about the same as that shown two years ago—2,209. The further diminution in immigrants from Japan, amounting to 3,930, as already suggested, is to be accounted for by the war between that country and Russia. Another reason, and one of special importance, for the decreases from these two countries is the medical inspection at the ports of foreign embarkation in Asia, which, as shown in the last annual report, has resulted in the detection of a relatively very large proportion of persons afflicted with trachoma, and their consequent inability to secure transportation to the United States.

European Turkey shows an increase of 198, Turkey in Asia of 922, and the unmentioned countries of Asia 2,964, so that there appears a prospect of the exploiting of the Orient as a source of supply for immigration, a field as practically inexhaustible as it is, as yet, virgin to the activities of the transportation agent.

Table II also shows that there were during the year 33,256 aliens who were landed to proceed to foreign countries, representing an increase in this class over the figures for last year of 5,412. The total aliens, therefore, admitted at our ports during the year reached the sum of 1,059,755.

TABLE III.—REPORT OF ALIENS (EXCLUSIVE OF ALIENS IN TRANSIT) ADMITTED AND DEBARRED AT THE PORTS OF THE UNITED STATES AND CANADA, FOR THE YEAR END-ING JUNE 30, 1905, SHOWING THE RACE OR PEOPLE TO WHICH THEY BELONG.

ADMITTED.

Race or people.	Male.	Female.	Total.	Under 14 years.	14 to 44 years.	45 years and over.
African (black)	2,325	1,273	3,598	433	2,974	191
Armenian	1,339	539	1,878	246	1,529	103
Bohemian and Moravian	6,662	5,095	11,757	2,620	8,442	695
Bulgarian, Servian, and Montenegrin	5,562	261	5,823	97	5,529	197
Chinese	1,883	88	1,971	28	1,666	277
Croatian and Slovenian	30,253	4,851	35,104	1,383	32,470	1,251
Cuban	4,925	2,334	7,259	1,346	5,225	688
Dalmatian, Bosnian, and Herzegovin-ian	2,489	150	2,639	62	2,450	127
Dutch and Flemish	5,693	2,805	8,498	1,699	6,085	714
East Indian	137	8	145	3	122	20
English	31,965	18,900	50,865	6,956	36,726	7,183
Filipino	4	1	5	....	4	1
Finnish	11,907	5,105	17,012	1,483	15,047	482
French	6,705	4,642	11,347	1,121	8,825	1,401
German	49,647	32,713	82,360	11,469	64,441	6,450
Greek	11,586	558	12,144	446	11,523	175
Hebrew	82,076	47,834	129,910	28,553	95,964	5,393
Irish	24,640	29,626	54,266	2,580	48,562	3,124
Italian (north)	31,695	8,235	39,930	3,569	34,561	1,800
Italian (south)	155,007	31,383	186,390	16,915	159,024	10,451
Japanese	9,810	1,211	11,021	124	10,588	309
Korean	4,506	423	4,929	325	4,557	47
Lithuanian	13,842	4,762	18,604	1,474	16,875	255

CHART I.
FOR FURTHER INFORMATION SEE PAGES 162 AND 163

BUREAU OF IMMIGRATION.

PROPORTION OF ARRIVALS AT SEAPORTS DEBARRED FROM LANDING, PROPORTION OF LANDED AFTERWARD RETURNED.

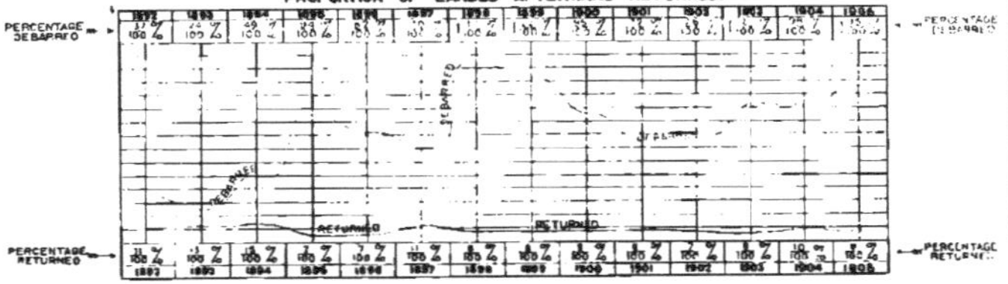

PERCENTAGE DEBARRED

PERCENTAGE RETURNED

TABLE SHOWING NUMBER DEBARRED AND CAUSES THEREFOR, NUMBER RETURNED AFTER LANDING AND NUMBER OF ARRIVALS (UPON WHICH THE ABOVE DIAGRAM IS BASED)

TABLE III.—REPORT OF ALIENS (EXCLUSIVE OF ALIENS IN TRANSIT) ADMITTED AND DEBARRED AT THE PORTS OF THE UNITED STATES AND CANADA, ETC.—Continued.

ADMITTED.

Race or people.	Male.	Female.	Total.	Under 14 years.	14 to 44 years.	45 years and over.
Magyar	34,242	11,788	46,030	3,864	39,926	2,240
Mexican	152	75	227	29	169	29
Pacific Islander	13	4	17	1	15	1
Polish	72,452	29,985	102,437	9,867	89,914	2,656
Portuguese	2,992	1,863	4,855	1,035	3,381	439
Roumanian	7,244	574	7,818	153	7,293	372
Russian	2,700	1,046	3,746	591	2,988	167
Ruthenian (Russniak)	10,820	3,653	14,473	661	13,321	491
Scandinavian (Norwegians, Danes, and Swedes)	37,202	25,082	62,284	6,597	52,226	3,461
Scotch	10,472	5,672	16,144	2,270	12,109	1,765
Slovak	38,038	14,330	52,368	4,582	45,882	1,904
Spanish	4,724	866	5,590	403	4,612	575
Spanish-American	1,146	512	1,658	223	1,232	203
Syrian	3,248	1,574	4,822	742	3,843	237
Turkish	2,082	63	2,145	45	2,073	27
Welsh	1,549	982	2,531	464	1,726	341
West Indian (except Cuban)	892	656	1,548	187	1,209	152
All other peoples	288	63	351	22	311	18
Total	724,914	301,585	1,026,499	114,668	855,419	56,412

Race or people.	Illiteracy, 14 years and over.		Immigrants bringing—		Total amount of money shown.	Have been in the United States before.
	Can read but can not write.	Can neither read nor write.	$50 or over.	Less than $50.		
African (black)	18	481	456	1,864	$88,016	1,443
Armenian	3	307	220	1,110	55,784	188
Bohemian and Moravian	8	147	1,206	6,347	331,517	668
Bulgarian, Servian, and Montenegrin	12	2,213	177	5,379	101,739	391
Chinese	3	95	222	1,517	39,697	1,117
Croatian and Slovenian	87	12,788	1,221	31,710	539,337	7,068
Cuban	2	456	2,053	1,544	289,730	4,942
Dalmatian, Bosnian, and Herzegovinian	6	985	200	2,315	55,575	309
Dutch and Flemish	14	349	2,171	3,182	453,165	1,455
East Indian		17	70	55	13,550	29
English	60	493	21,265	15,563	2,924,080	15,558
Filipino		1	4	1	206	3
Finnish	161	118	1,286	13,432	362,047	2,657
French	4	276	5,019	3,319	981,093	3,657
German	180	2,813	17,847	41,648	3,600,845	13,444
Greek	10	2,666	1,152	10,310	331,871	1,021
Hebrew	807	22,770	7,091	59,319	1,824,617	2,698
Irish	130	1,445	6,851	37,161	1,421,682	14,658
Italian (north)	25	5,058	4,893	28,780	1,169,990	8,240
Italian (south)	97	95,407	8,922	146,868	3,127,207	39,204
Japanese		4,287	3,476	5,905	416,395	1,515
Korean		1,925	27	80	3,931	18
Lithuanian	2,133	7,606	531	14,953	224,219	767
Magyar	78	4,828	1,541	37,064	695,108	6,575
Mexican	2	17	108	37	14,266	109
Pacific Islander		3	7	9	628	7
Polish	3,519	33,167	2,534	82,653	1,352,230	9,220
Portuguese	3	2,543	537	2,789	125,962	998
Roumanian	14	2,194	103	7,269	110,068	605
Russian	30	996	519	2,052	133,576	259
Ruthenian (Russniak)	139	8,513	148	13,144	179,889	2,243
Scandinavian (Norwegians, Danes, and Swedes)	159	157	7,139	42,915	1,604,205	12,773
Scotch	17	75	5,744	6,168	810,678	3,945
Slovak	430	11,554	1,169	44,429	818,207	12,532
Spanish	23	503	2,143	2,496	336,105	2,327
Spanish-American	4	39	1,070	141	157,196	733
Syrian	11	2,178	784	2,533	211,485	744
Turkish	6	1,267	103	1,958	53,634	132
Welsh	11	62	847	911	130,148	680
West Indian (except Cuban)		35	695	506	96,242	563
All other peoples		50	102	129	23,152	69
Total	8,209	230,882	111,652	679,565	25,159,012	175,624

TABLE III.—REPORT OF ALIENS (EXCLUSIVE OF ALIENS IN TRANSIT) ADMITTED AND DEBARRED AT THE PORTS OF THE UNITED STATES AND CANADA, ETC.—Continued.

Race or people.	DEBARRED.									
	Idiots.	Insane persons.	Paupers, or likely to become public charges.	Loathsome or dangerous contagious diseases.	Convicts.	Contract laborers.	Assisted immigrants.	Anarchists.	Persons who procure or attempt to bring in prostitutes.	Polygamists.
African (black)			107		1	13				
Armenian			25	50		5				
Bohemian and Moravian		1	38	8		5				
Bulgarian, Servian, and Montenegrin			314	19		62				
Chinese		1	9	74		3				
Croatian and Slovenian			263	88		32	2			
Cuban		1	22	4		11				
Dalmatian, Bosnian, and Herzegovinian			41	3		13				
Dutch and Flemish	2	1	51	7		5				
East Indian			12			1				
English	4	9	328	28		58	2		1	
Finnish	2	1	33	46		4				
French		2	94	9	1	23			1	
German	5	8	420	100		60				
Greek			198	22	1	60				
Hebrew	10	10	1,208	353		33	8			
Irish	4	13	175	28		15				
Italian (north)		2	169	41		42				
Italian (south)	6	19	1,578	247	35	205	4	1		
Japanese		1	238	285		13			2	
Korean			4	18						
Lithuanian	2	1	48	92		8				
Magyar			427	103		19				
Mexican			7	8						
Polish		4	444	204		125	1			
Portuguese			30	7		1				
Roumanian			388	14		111				
Russian		3	66	27		1				
Ruthenian (Russniak)	1	1	186	14		13				
Scandinavian (Norwegians, Danes, and Swedes)	2	9	152	43		14				
Scotch		2	77	10		21				
Slovak			275	66		47				
Spanish		1	66	6		63				
Spanish American			13	4		1				
Syrian			124	155		59	2			2
Turkish			46	9		5				1
Welsh		1	12	1		13				
West Indian (except Cuban)		1	20			1				
All other peoples			195	5						
Grand total	38	92	7,898	2,198	39	1,164	19	1	4	3

CHART 2
FOR FURTHER INFORMATION SEE PAGES 102 AND 103.

BUREAU OF IMMIGRATION
F.P. SARGENT, Commissioner-Gen.

ALIEN CONTRACT LABORERS

DENIED ADMISSION TO THE UNITED STATES

(CITIZENS, FOREIGN CONTIGUOUS TERRITORY NOT INCLUDED)

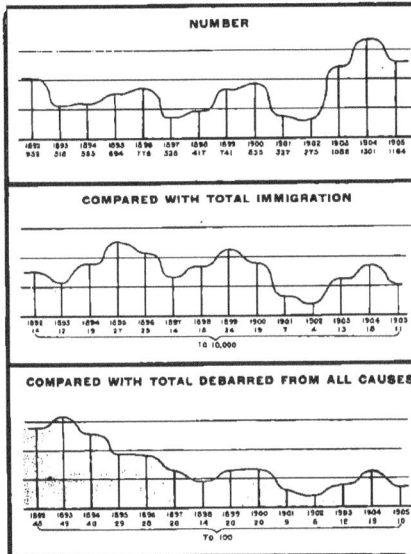

NUMBER

1892	1893	1894	1895	1896	1897	1898	1899	1900	1901	1902	1903	1904	1905
935	516	583	694	778	528	417	741	635	327	273	1088	1301	1164

COMPARED WITH TOTAL IMMIGRATION

1892	1893	1894	1895	1896	1897	1898	1899	1900	1901	1902	1903	1904	1905
14	12	19	27	25	14	18	24	19	7	4	13	18	11

To 10,000

COMPARED WITH TOTAL DEBARRED FROM ALL CAUSES

1892	1893	1894	1895	1896	1897	1898	1899	1900	1901	1902	1903	1904	1905
48	49	48	29	28	20	14	20	20	9	6	12	19	10

To 100

TABLE III.—REPORT OF ALIENS (EXCLUSIVE OF ALIENS IN TRANSIT) ADMITTED AND DEBARRED AT THE PORTS OF THE UNITED STATES AND CANADA, ETC.—Continued.

Race or people.	DEBARRED—Continued.					Returned in one year after landing.	Returned in two years after landing.	Returned in three years after landing.	Relieved in hospital.
	Prostitutes.	Chinese exclusion act.	Carrying concealed weapons.	Fraudulent papers.	Violating law.				
African (black)	1						9	1	3
Armenian									78.
Bohemian and Moravian						5	10	3	104
Bulgarian, Servian, and Montenegrin							2	1	37
Chinese		394						6	2
Croatian and Slovenian						1	3	2	128
Cuban	4						3	2	
Dalmatian, Bosnian, and Herzegovinian							2		18
Dutch and Flemish						6	2	1	41
East Indian									3
English	5					9	23	11	144
Finnish						8	18	4	89
French	6					2	12	30	48
German	2					4	94	33	747
Greek						1	8	1	70
Hebrew	1					9	68	15	1,534
Irish					1	2	57	4	243
Italian (north)						2	7	2	158
Italian (south)	1		2	1		6	60	14	1,290
Japanese	1			1		2		53	2
Korean									1
Lithuanian						1	3		269
Magyar						9	20	7	363
Mexican	1					1	1	13	2
Polish						9	40	8	991
Portuguese						1			26
Roumanian							2		47
Russian						1	1		69
Ruthenian (Russniak)							7		115
Scandinavian (Norwegians, Danes, and Swedes)						4	39	13	253
Scotch						1	8	1	75
Slovak						1	6		491
Spanish	1					1	6		23
Spanish American	1							1	6
Syrian						8	2	2	200
Turkish						1	2		17
Welsh						3	1		8
West Indian (except Cuban)							3		17
All other peoples									74
Grand total	24	394	2	2	1	98	519	228	7,776

Of the 1,026,499 alien arrivals during the past year, exclusive of the 33,256 who passed through and out of this country, Table III shows that 175,624 had been here formerly. The total was divided as to sex into 724,914 males and 301,585 females; as to age into 114,668 under 14 years, 855,419 ranging from 14 to 44, inclusive, and 56,412 who were 45 years of age or over. There were 230,882 who could neither read nor write and 8,209 who were unable to write but could read, the remainder, according to their own statements, being sufficiently educated to both read and write. Those who brought $50 each or more, numbered 111,652, while 679,565 brought amounts of less than $50 each, the unreported balance of 235,282 representing minors or dependents, who brought no money. The total amount of money shown by alien arrivals was $25,159,012, or $4,264,629 in excess of the amount brought by immigrants last year.

Simply as an indication of the respective financial capacity of the different races of aliens to provide for themselves it is interesting to note that the 50,865 English brought $2,924,080, while the 46,030

Magyars had but $695,108; the 54,266 Irish had $1,421,682, and the 129,910 Hebrews showed $1,824,617; the 82,360 Germans possessed $3,600,845, and the 186,390 South Italians, $3,127,207; the 11,347 French, $931,093, and the 35,104 Croatians and Slovenians, $539,337; the 16,144 Scotch, $810,678, and the 52,368 Slovaks, $818,207.

From Table III it also appears that a total of 11,480 aliens was refused admission for the causes shown in the accompanying statement, in which, for purposes of comparison, are given also the corresponding figures for last year.

Cause.	1904.	1905.	Cause.	1904.	1905.
Idiocy	16	38	Procurers	3	4
Insanity	33	92	Assisted aliens	38	19
Pauperism	4,798	7,898	Contract laborers	1,501	1,164
Cantagious diseases	1,560	2,198	Anarchists	1	1
Conviction of crime	35	39			
Polygamy		3	Total	7,994	11,480
Imported for prostitution	9	24			

Omitting consideration of those who were rejected under the provisions of the Chinese-exclusion laws and who therefore do not properly come within a discussion of the question of the general immigration laws, it will be seen that the exclusions constitute about 1 per cent of the total arrivals.

The most significant feature of this statement is the large increase in the number of idiots, insane persons, and paupers during the past year, which, coupled with an increase of 25 per cent in the number of diseased aliens, justifies the Bureau in directing attention elsewhere herein to the flagrant and willful disregard by the ocean carriers of the laws for the regulation of their business of securing alien passengers destined to the United States.

Below is repeated the tabulated statement of rejections since 1891, which was first published last year, with the figures for the year to which this report refers added:

REPORT OF IMMIGRANTS REFUSED ADMISSION AT SEAPORTS, SHOWING ALSO THOSE RETURNED IN ONE YEAR AFTER LANDING, UNDER THE PROVISIONS OF THE ALIEN CONTRACT-LABOR LAWS AND THE LAWS REGULATING IMMIGRATION, DURING THE TWELVE YEARS, 1892 TO 1905, INCLUSIVE.

Year.	Immigrants.	Debarred.												Returned in 1 year after landing.	Returned in 2 years after landing.	Returned in 3 years after landing.
		Idiots.	Insane persons.	Paupers, or likely to become public charges.	Loathsome or dangerous contagious diseases.	Convicts.	Polygamists.	Anarchists.	Prostitutes.	Persons who procure or attempt to bring in prostitutes.	Assisted immigrants.	Contract laborers.	Total debarred.			
1892	579,663	4	17	1,002	80	26			80		23	932	2,164	637		
1893	439,730	3	8	431	81	12						518	1,053	577		
1894	285,631	4	5	802	15	8			2			553	1,389	417		
1895	258,536	6		1,714		4					1	694	2,419	177		
1896	343,267	1		2,010	2							776	2,799	238		
1897	230,832	1	6	1,277	1	1					3	328	1,617	263		
1898	229,299	1	12	2,261	258	2					79	417	3,030	199		
1899	311,715	1	19	2,599	348	8					82	741	3,798	263		
1900	448,572	1	32	2,974	393	4			7		2	833	4,246	356		
1901	487,918	6	16	2,798	309	7			3		50	327	3,516	363		
1902	648,743	7	27	3,944	709	9			3			275	4,974	465		
1903	857,046	1	23	5,812	1,773	51	1		13		9	1,086	8,769	547		
1904	812,870	16	38	4,798	1,560	35		1	9	3	38	1,501	7,994	300		479
1905	1,026,499	38	92	7,898	2,198	39	3	1	24	4	19	1,164	11,480	98	519	228

Especial attention is directed to the arrest and deportation during the year of 845 aliens found to be in this country in violation of law. This was effected with small expense and without invoking the tedious, elaborate, and expensive machinery of the courts, in striking contrast to the difficulties, adverse criticism, and cost involved in relieving the United States of the unlawful presence, as shown further on in the financial statement, of 621 Chinese laborers, at a cost of $67,730.61, exclusive of the expenses incurred in their trial before the courts.

An interesting and important item of information shown by Table III is that during the year 7,786 aliens received medical treatment in hospital, who were distributed, as regards race, as follows:

Hebrews	1,534	Irish	243
Italians (south)	1,290	Syrians	200
Poles	991	Italians (north)	158
Germans	747	Croatians and Slovenians	128
Slovaks	491	Ruthenians	115
Magyars	363	All others	1,004
Lithuanians	269		
Scandinavians	253	Total	7,786

The racial elements of the total immigration for the year is shown in the subjoined statement taken from Table III:

Italians (south)	186,390	Lithuanians	18,604
Hebrews	129,910	Finnish	17,012
Poles	102,137	Scotch	16,144
Germans	82,360	Ruthenians	14,473
Scandinavians	62,284	Greeks	12,144
Irish	54,266	Bohemians and Moravians	11,757
Slovaks	52,368	French	11,347
English	50,865	Japanese	11,021
Magyars	46,030	All others	72,353
Italians (north)	39,930		
Croatians and Slovenians	35,104	Total	1,026,499

TABLE III A.—REPORT OF ALIENS REFUSED ADMISSION FROM FOREIGN CONTIGUOUS TERRITORY, TO THE UNITED STATES, UNDER THE PROVISIONS OF THE ALIEN CONTRACT-LABOR LAWS AND THE LAWS REGULATING IMMIGRATION, FOR THE YEAR ENDING JUNE 30, 1905.

Port	Total debarred.	Persons who procure or attempt to bring in prostitutes.	Illegal entry.	Gamblers.	Anarchists.	To prevent separation of family.	Assisted immigrants.	No certificate.	Contract laborers.	Women for immoral purposes.	Convicts.	Other debarring cases.	Loathsome or dangerous contagious diseases.	Paupers, or likely to become public charges.	Insane persons.	Idiots.
STATIONS HAVING BOARDS OF SPECIAL INQUIRY.																
Black Rock, N.Y.	27								8	1			1	17	1	
Blaine, Wash.a	6								1				3	4	3	2
Detroit, Mich.	63								31	4				22		1
Duluth, Minn	4								2	2				2		
Estevan, Canada	2						1			1						
Montreal, Canada	27					15								4		
Niagara Falls, N.Y.	48					6			5	1	1		6	29		
Northport, Wash.	4								5							
Port Huron, Mich.	58											3	3	13	1	
Quebec, Canada.	3								37							
Sault Ste. Marie, Mich.	43					1			21	2			3	22	3	1
Sumas, Wash.	9					4			1				2	2		
Vanceboro, Me.	67					14			20				2	37		
Winnipeg, Canada.	23								6	1	1		1	6		1
Yarmouth, Nova Scotia.	9															
CANADIAN BORDER STATIONS.																
Alburg, Vt.	28							28						7		
Blaine, Wash.	26							19	1			1	1	6		
Cape Vincent, N.Y.	36							27	1							
Charlotte, N.Y.	1															
Cornwall, Ontario.	2							2								
Deloraine, Manitoba.	12							12								
Fort Francis, Ontario	11							8						2		
Gateway, Mont.	10							9		1						
Malone, N.Y.	9							9								
Morristown, N.Y.	30							17				2		13	2	1
Neche, N.Dak.	143							135	3					3		
North Stratford, N.H.	38							18	3				3	17		
Newport, Vt.	44							30	1				1	12		

Station																	Total
Oswego, N. Y.																	3
Ogdensburg, N. Y.																	65
Pemoina, N. Dak.																	107
Rouses Point, N. Y.																	64
Rainy River, Ontario																	31
Warroad, Minn																	13
St. Albans, Vt.																	16
Swanton, Vt.																	15
Total	7	10	297	21	6	2	15	169	b524	1	40				1		b1,092
MEXICAN BORDER STATIONS.																	
Brownsville, Tex			89														172
Del Rio, Tex			12														13
Douglas, Ariz			182														200
Eagle Pass, Tex			1,412														1,569
El Paso, Tex			1,120														1,583
Laredo, Tex			532							294							671
Naco, Ariz			392														411
Nogales, Ariz			109														143
Total	7	11	3,848	135		8	120	281	1	293		1	1	4		2	4,712
Total border rejections	14	21	4,145	156	6	10	135	450	b525	294	40	1	1	4	1	2	b5,804

a Board organized October, 1904.
b Of the number reported as rejected, cause "no certificate," 152 were subsequently admitted by the board of special inquiry.

The total rejections at each of the ports in Canada and along the Canadian boundary shown in the foregoing table will appear to disagree with similar data given in the tables included in the report of the commissioner of immigration at Montreal.   This disagreement is due to the fact that the figures in the foregoing table represent those aliens who are subjects for the collection of the head tax, and do not therefore include Canadians.   This is because of the uniform practice, due to circumstances narrated in former reports, of supplying statistical information in regard to such aliens only coming from foreign contiguous countries as/are subjects for the head tax.   The tables of the commissioner at Montreal, however, embrace all rejections, including those not subjects for the head tax, but who are in other respects within the provisions of the immigration laws.

In regular order are subjoined the various tables giving statistical information in regard to the total immigration for the fiscal year, as indicated in the headings to those tables, respectively.

It should be borne in mind that neither the information in regard to occupations nor that giving destinations is conclusive of the facts stated.   The destination is taken from the avowed purposes of the aliens upon that point, which, even if true, are subject to change.   As respects the occupations given they merely represent the pursuits followed by the aliens in their own country and are of value in calculating the capabilities of the arrivals, but doubtless these occupations in many instances are abandoned on arrival in the United States and others are pursued.

TABLE IV.—REPORT OF ALIENS (EXCLUSIVE OF ALIENS IN TRANSIT) ADMITTED INTO THE UNITED STATES, BY MONTHS, FOR TWELVE MONTHS ENDING JUNE 30, 1904 AND 1905.

Month.	1904.			1905.		
	Males.	Females.	Total.	Males.	Females.	Total.
July...	43,926	23,449	67,375	37,008	20,783	57,791
August......................................	40,958	23,364	64,322	36,645	23,132	59,777
September	46,840	31,490	78,330	39,204	33,562	72,766
October.....................................	51,172	30,344	81,516	42,452	32,873	75,325
November	43,917	24,110	68,027	46,630	24,407	71,037
December...................................	28,724	15,672	44,396	44,369	18,288	62,657
January.....................................	19,528	9,000	28,528	42,527	13,709	56,236
February	24,307	9,660	33,967	52,528	14,577	67,105
March	62,054	16,171	78,225	101,756	25,152	126,908
April..	69,338	21,985	91,323	107,036	30,014	137,050
May...	69,592	31,836	101,428	95,432	32,079	127,511
June..	48,744	26,689	75,433	79,327	33,009	112,336
Total..................	549,100	263,770	812,870	724,914	301,585	1,026,499

TABLE V.—REPORT OF ALIENS (EXCLUSIVE OF ALIENS IN TRANSIT) ADMITTED AT THE PORTS OF THE UNITED STATES FOR THE YEAR ENDING JUNE 30, 1905, SHOWING THE COUNTRIES WHENCE THEY CAME AND THE RACES OR PEOPLES TO WHICH THEY BELONG—Continued.

Country.	Korean.	Lithuanian.	Magyar.	Mexican.	Pacific Islanders.	Polish.	Portuguese.	Roumanian.	Russian.	Ruthenian or Russniak.	Scandinavian (Norwegians, Danes, and Swedes).	Scotch.	Slovak.	Spanish.	Spanish American.	Syrian.	Turkish.	Welsh.	West Indian (except Cuban).	All other peoples.	Total aliens.
Austria-Hungary		30	45,871			50,785	2	7,261	82	14,260	38	1	52,282	1	1		8			10	275,698
Austria		23	571			50,450	1	94	79	10,982	36	1	1,273	1	1		8			5	111,990
Hungary		7	45,300			335	1	7,167	3	3,268	2		51,009							5	163,703
Belgium		5	13			4			9	2	40	3		2	3					1	5,302
Denmark				11		13		17	5		8,787	2	10				20		2	16	8,970
France, including Corsica		34	17		6	19	9	17	43		57	13		98	48	27	12		21	11	10,168
German Empire			24			3,858	2	5	40	4	173	13	13	8	5	1	46	27			40,574
Greece						2															10,515
Italy, including Sicily and Sardinia		1	2			4		4	3	2	2	4	7	2	6	1	1		1	3	221,479
Netherlands		1				21			11			1			1	2	8				4,954
Norway										20	25,008					5					25,064
Portugal, including Cape Verde and Azore islands			11			3	4,680	423	2	1		4		15	3						5,028
Roumania		1																	1		4,437
Russian Empire and Finland		17,649	4			47,224		4	3,278	178	690	1	11				1		1	1	184,897
Russian Empire		17,649	4			47,223		4	3,269	178	82	1	11				1		1	1	167,928
Finland						1			9		608										16,969
Servia, Bulgaria, and Montenegro								27													2,043
Spain, including Canary and Balearic islands			1	6			5		1		1		13	2,405	1	3	49		19	2	2,600
Sweden			1			3	1	1			26,442	1		6	83	3	1				26,691
Switzerland		1				2			3		11	2		1	1			1		2	4,269
Turkey in Europe			3					27	4			1	4	7	2	75	1,664			11	4,542

TABLE V.—REPORT OF ALIENS (EXCLUSIVE OF ALIENS IN TRANSIT) ADMITTED AT THE PORTS OF THE UNITED STATES FOR THE YEAR ENDING JUNE 30, 1905, SHOWING THE COUNTRIES WHENCE THEY CAME AND THE RACES OR PEOPLES TO WHICH THEY BELONG—Continued.

Country	Korean	Lithuanian	Magyar	Mexico	Pacific Islanders	Polish	Portuguese	Roumanian	Russian	Ruthenian or Russeniak	Scandinavian (Norwegian, Danes, and Swedes)	Scotch	Slovak	Spanish	Spanish-American	Syrian	Turkish	Welsh	West Indian (except Cuban)	All other peoples	Total aliens
United Kingdom		868	57	5		444	9	17	169	7	533	15,641	11	339	32	30	11	2,466	21	14	127,134
England		291	56	5		292	9	17	152	7	472	416	9	326	25	30	9	135	20	12	64,709
Ireland		17				2			2		18	53		2	7			7		1	52,945
Scotland		560	1			149			14		32	15,163	2	2			2	8	1	1	16,977
Wales						1			1		11	9		9				2,316			2,508
Europe, not specified							10							3							13
Total Europe		18,590	46,004	24	6	102,382	4,658	7,804	3,652	14,464	61,782	15,677	52,352	2,886	186	148	1,822	2,495	65	72	974,273
China	1										13	4					1				2,166
Japan											12	7					5			1	10,331
India												10				1	11			7	190
Turkey in Asia																4,086	266			38	6,157
Other Asia	4,920	1							14		1	1		1	4	30	16	1		85	5,081
Total Asia	4,921	1							14		26	22		1	4	4,117	299	1		131	28,925
Africa		10	4	4		5	7	1	9		12	10	1	11	1	23	3	2	6	31	757
Australia, Tasmania, and New Zealand		1			1	1	2	1	16		69	160	9	6	1	4		16	1	8	2,091
Philippine Islands					10	1			5		10	6		1	6						39
Pacific islands, not specified																				4	36
British North America	2		3	8		8	1	8	6		129	149	1	12	23	7	1	9	3	14	2,168
British Honduras							5		28		2	1		65	58	2	13	2	5	14	123
Other Central America						1	8		10		21	11		355	509	223	2	1	26	12	1,072
Mexico	3		5	147		9	97	4	6		59	43	5	129	694	139	3	1	6		2,687
South America	3	2	12			25	61			9	32	21		2,118	176	148		1	62		2,576
West Indies			1	44		5	12				125	43		3		11		4	1,373	65	16,641
All other countries											27	1									161
Grand total	4,929	18,604	46,030	227	17	102,437	4,855	7,818	3,746	14,473	62,294	16,144	52,368	5,590	1,658	4,822	2,145	2,581	1,548	351	1,026,499

TABLE VI.—REPORT OF ALIENS ADMITTED INTO THE UNITED STATES DURING THE YEAR ENDING JUNE 30, 1905.

Country.	Sex and number of aliens admitted.			Aliens in transit.	Grand total.
	Males.	Females.	Total.		
Austria-Hungary...............................	197,557	78,136	275,693	2,797	278,490
Austria..	76,188	35,802	111,990	1,509	113,499
Hungary	121,369	42,334	163,703	1,288	164,991
Belgium.......................................	3,554	1,748	5,302	214	5,516
Denmark......................................	5,689	3,281	8,970	74	9,044
France, including Corsica.....................	6,007	4,161	10,168	1,520	11,688
German Empire	23,348	17,226	40,574	1,001	41,575
Greece...	10,016	499	10,515	133	10,648
Italy, including Sicily and Sardinia.............	182,718	38,761	221,479	3,833	225,312
Netherlands...................................	3,219	1,735	4,954	129	5,083
Norway	15,852	9,212	25,064	268	25,332
Portugal, including Cape Verde and Azore islands.	3,151	1,877	5,028	21	5,049
Roumania......................................	2,264	2,173	4,437	116	4,553
Russian Empire and Finland......................	127,871	57,026	184,897	2,482	187,379
Russian Empire	116,045	51,883	167,928	2,289	170,217
Finland	11,826	5,143	16,969	193	17,162
Servia, Bulgaria, and Montenegro	1,990	53	2,043	24	2,067
Spain, including Canary and Balearic islands	2,156	444	2,600	463	3,063
Sweden..	14,411	12,180	26,591	237	26,828
Switzerland	2,694	1,575	4,269	90	4,359
Turkey in Europe	4,400	142	4,542	284	4,826
United Kingdom	77,714	59,420	137,134	8,659	145,793
England.......................................	41,276	23,433	64,709	6,911	71,620
Ireland..	23,841	29,104	52,945	545	53,490
Scotland.......................................	11,047	5,930	16,977	1,114	18,091
Wales	1,550	953	2,503	89	2,592
Europe, not specified...........................	9	4	13	....	13
Total Europe...............................	684,620	289,653	974,273	22,345	996,618
China	2,021	145	2,166	1,354	3,520
Japan	9,105	1,226	10,331	794	11,125
India..	155	35	190	37	227
Turkey in Asia.................................	4,235	1,922	6,157	324	6,481
Other Asia	4,632	449	5,081	16	5,097
Total Asia.................................	20,148	3,777	23,925	2,525	26,450
Africa	601	156	757	93	850
Australia, Tasmania, and New Zealand...........	1,425	666	2,091	562	2,653
Philippine Islands.............................	36	3	39	1	40
Pacific islands, not specified....................	28	8	36	47	83
British North America	1,817	351	2,168	2,265	4,433
British Honduras	77	46	123	43	166
Other Central America.........................	751	321	1,072	539	1,611
Mexico	2,178	459	2,637	1,263	3,900
South America	1,866	710	2,576	836	3,412
West Indies....................................	11,264	5,377	16,641	2,691	19,332
All other countries............................	103	58	161	46	207
Grand total...............................	724,914	301,585	1,026,499	33,256	1,059,755

TABLE VII.—REPORT OF ALIENS (EXCLUSIVE OF ALIENS IN TRANSIT) ADMITTED INTO THE UNITED STATES FOR THE YEAR ENDING JUNE 30, 1905, SHOWING RACE OR PEOPLE, BY DESTINATION.

Rank	Destination	African (black)	Armenian	Bohemian and Moravian	Bulgarian, Servian, and Montenegrin	Chinese	Croatian and Slovenian	Cuban	Dalmatian, Bosnian, and Herzegovinian	Dutch and Flemish	East Indian	English	Filipino	Finnish	French	German	Greek	Hebrew	Irish	Italian (north)	Italian (south)	Japanese
39	Alabama	43		1	2		11	62	12	4	1	100		4	30	39	49	107	16	45	83	
52	Alaska				12	5	12		23	3	1	11		19	10	5	4		6	1	1	10
45	Arizona			20	52		37	11		8	11	216		6	29	47	1	3	22	115	34	70
48	Arkansas			17	3		54	1		1		35	1	1	3	113	115	24	19	38	26	
8	California	29	1	39	67	1,016	224	7	301	109		2,468	1	316	1,021	1,583	90	341	994	824	1,081	2,022
21	Colorado		59	44	84	2	696	4	46	21		319	2	84	61	449	150	104	135	4,513	881	15
9	Connecticut	38	26	76	7	3	74	9	19	22		944		137	141	1,358	42	2,044	124	1,626	5,835	1
35	Delaware	1		2				1		2		225			2	32	87	55	159	93	389	1
38	District of Columbia	18		1	2			9		46		274		7	170	203	98	272	49	108	649	20
20	Florida	1,582	5	2			70	4,691	1	11		60		20	25	88	2	21	23	21	509	4
46	Georgia						1	17		4		92		10	9	56	87	131		16	5	1
11	Hawaii					205	1		72			88	2		6	28			6	2	2	6,692
41	Idaho					5			8			587			11	82			19	24	5	56
4	Illinois	17	63	3,258	709	6	4,109	3	246	4		2,587	1	25	478	7,614	1,504	5,480	2,381	3,663	6,685	
47	Indian Territory	1				1						28			5	8				6	59	
23	Indiana	1	1	26	231	4	401	11	13	219		331		326	140	789	95	199	195	227	298	1
15	Iowa	1		283	4	5	162		1	291		350			79	1,084	24	206	175	302	75	2
29	Kansas	1		95	1	12	339			353	1	264		56	338	1,109	17	18	95	206	113	
44	Kentucky	23			2	2	5			77		96		4	9	191	16	150	46	323	40	1
18	Louisiana	19		29	1	6	24	7	72	2		342		1	301	255	36	136	308	10	2,631	2
31	Maine		32			1	6	135	8	36		377		31	21	30	36	249	268	177	409	
22	Maryland	433	1	299		5	99	3	2	18		834		184	47	1,455	97	2,376	276	65	11,747	1
3	Massachusetts	1	659	64	39	12	22	25	6	25	3	377	1	3,198	559	1,018	110	9,097	220	59	660	4
10	Michigan		42	185	35	2	876	24	8	509	1	1,488		4,242	82	1,676	33	608	7	2,011	1,649	18
7	Minnesota	10	6	286	130	6	722		38	1,440		461		2,397	39	1,349	20	656	489	1,330	517	5
50	Mississippi	4			21	1	32		160	219	1	37		13	10	30	10	48	278	306	213	
14	Missouri		40	287			1,583	8	41	8	1	960		152	599	4,052	1	739	100	674	1,477	165
30	Montana		1	4	504	332	226	178		198		257		3	50	152	6	7	18	769	39	12
24	Nebraska		1	506	63	7	38		11	33	1	136		152	31	1,009	1,671	178	401	122	68	
40	Nevada					1	33		3	47	1	23		10	51	16		6		35	29	1
33	New Hampshire	1	20		15			8	11		1	226		9	14	66	6	226	3,386	262	113	
5	New Jersey	66	77	218	47	1	333	178	179	728	11	2,143		202	310	5,548	585	4,226	100	1,272	11,494	13
49	New Mexico			2	15		77	1		11	19	25		11	24	19	169	4	401	82	5	5
1	New York	1,040	500	2,047	557	104	2,762	1,820	642	1,595	31	15,747	1	268	4,723	21,416	3,154	83,724	19,688	9,733	81,572	256
51	North Carolina							12	12			56			1	13	9	22	4	6	3	

16	North Dakota			64			5			38		155		57	17	1,570	1	71	41	11	9	1
6	Ohio	2	5	1,378	1,358	4	3,912	7	147	109		1,418		612	187	7,382	153	2,169	806	861	6,230	7
43	Oklahoma		1	62	1			2				17				123	10	1	1	1		
32	Oregon		1	2	1	45	28		21.	39	2	146		242	38	207	53	76	62	74	94	279
2	Pennsylvania	58	88	1,015	1,468	13	15,505	66	253	191	10	6,560		625	924	13,717	692	13,477	7,468	7,554	43,078	17
54	Philippine Islands											3								1		
27	Porto Rico	104		1				100		16		47		97	41			2	16	29		
13	Rhode Island	65	244	14	2		1	4	1	77	1	1,776		41	203	153	76	622	1,190	196	2,422	
53	South Carolina			10				8			3	15		3	3	20	13	24	11	10	9	
25	South Dakota	1		64	27	3	52		38	90		116		136	3	679		24	29	45	6	
42	Tennessee	2			1	1	161	6		2		71		3	9	63	35	137	10	122	73	1
26	Texas	3		823	135	1	92	3	28	72		336		23	123	666	54	208	124	183	239	88
28	Utah		1		3	10	164			87		456		90	23	217	88	8	49	140	118	
34	Vermont	1		6	2		1			1	1	112		47	14	33	11	54	77	227	226	
36	Virginia	16	2	15	9		83	1	6	17		228		12	15	104	84	157	68	64	105	1
17	Washington	1		20	32	155	325		50	75	43	719		596	155	686	127	63	145	456	784	1,200
19	West Virginia			51	179		901		217	20		212			23	308	101	42	45	421	2,987	2
12	Wisconsin		2	394	28	1	754	1	2	333	1	235		429	19	3,224	242	696	117	290	584	2
37	Wyoming			31	17		73		7	1		82		235	8	27	5	1	18	130	21	
55	Tourists	4		5	1	1	1	4		33	4	1,408			57	208	3	7	80	9	20	41
	Grand total	3,596	1,878	11,757	5,823	1,971	35,104	7,259	2,689	8,498	145	50,865	5	17,012	11,347	82,360	12,144	129,910	54,266	39,980	186,390	11,021

Table VII.—Report of Aliens (Exclusive of Aliens in Transit) Admitted into the United States for the Year ending June 30, 1905, showing Race or People, by Destination—Continued.

Rank	Destination	Korean	Lithuanian	Magyar	Mexican	Pacific Islander	Polish	Portuguese	Roumanian	Russian	Ruthenian or Russniak	Scandinavian (Norwegians, Danes, and Swedes)	Scotch	Slovak	Spanish	Spanish-American	Syrian	Turkish	Welsh	West Indian (except Cuban)	All other peoples	Total aliens
39	Alabama	1	2	2	3		4			1		169	19	16	33	13	37	1	4	17		912
52	Alaska									1		31	11	2				1				152
45	Arizona		4	3	69		17	2		11		39	22	5	56	1	3	3	1		2	854
48	Arkansas			26				2				9	17	21		2	5					432
8	California	22	13	1,861	1	12	65	901	8	431		1,582	601	27	399	201	20	10	9	11	50	20,823
21	Colorado		12	9			37		90	108	2	383	186	57	1	1	10		55	10	15	4,491
9	Connecticut		1,175	17			4,697	34	6	13	3	1,417	232	1,296	6	3	105	29	31	9		26,174
35	Delaware	3	9				436	10	3	2		14	9	3				1	10		8	1,231
38	Dist. Columbia											57	42	17	48		15					2,380
20	Florida		2	4	1	2	7	9		1		68	29	2	1,289	50	28		2	139		8,972
46	Georgia						2	1				17	19	1	3	7	15		1	1		518
11	Hawaii	4,892					1					9	36						6	1	20	11,978
41	Idaho											159	38								7	645
4	Illinois		8,440	1,354	14		13,662	3	157	227	362	7,770	933	3,777	150	9	97	95	118			72,770
47	Indian Territory		15	11			13			2		8	14	7			5					6,742
28	Indiana		84	1,025			643	5	618	2		186	214	323	19		107	131	49			5,412
15	Iowa		29	13			43	6	5	4		2,059	176	18	3		22		44			3,370
29	Kansas		7	9	2		118			3		264	84	36	3		9		19			681
44	Kentucky			12			5			2		14	12	1			26					5,101
18	Louisiana			11	2			7		15		273	27	4	20		142					2,798
31	Maine	1	1	18			125	2				272	172	81	2		65		2	14	7	8,511
22	Maryland		169	115			1,310		1	174	230	152	171	204	160		11		9	4	3	
3	Massachusetts		354	121			8,388	2,909	2	222	8	4,335	2,183	321	10		694	511	95	11	1	72,151
10	Michigan		2,464	719			3,558	4	81	20	22	1,798	358	293			156	39	20	82	25	21,897
7	Minnesota		174	67			814	16	19	11	3	8,694	170	188	65		17	17	19	5	2	17,089
50	Mississippi		12						40	12		318	2	2								
14	Missouri		2	415	3		13		29	63	5	514	227	590			44	2	1	8		17,142
30	Montana				1	1						969	112	13			130					18,653
24	Nebraska		77	11			141			1		24	41	4			6		54			3,410
40	Nevada		26	23	19							281	5							1		687
33	New Hampshire		187							1			76		9		16	65		2	1	3,001
5	New Jersey		865	7,177			9,124	17	338	102	1,666	1,730	874	4,871	213		45	217	24	3	1	57,258
49	New Mexico				8		2		1			19	8		168	150	105	1	18	49	19	385
1	New York	3	2,384	8,076	99	1	18,839	412	415	1,302	2,275	12,662	4,320	6,254	1,785	888	1,474	353	391	863	129	315,510
51	North Carolina			4						1	1	7	21	1	2		20		1	3	2	188

																						Total
16	North Dakota		12	34			108	1	38	29	19	3,130	106	7			14		8			4	5,546
6	Ohio		280	8,193	2		3,814	21	3,565	55	522	435	476	4,664			246	158	163	2		3	49,351
43	Oklahoma						8					7	3				21					2	260
32	Oregon		1	1			8			5		411	94	12	1		4		5	1		19	1,955
2	Pennsylvania		6,229	15,226	2		30,820	6	2,038	737	8,510	2,169	2,369	27,552	97	33	627	310	1,098	89			210,708
54	Philippine Islands												2										6
27	Porto Rico												6		163	1			190	7		1,630
13	Rhode Island		51	11			836	467	2	8	63	4	282	21	760		44	1	23	5	1		9,474
58	South Carolina						1			2		490	163		1		88	36	1				328
25	South Dakota			5			6			5		5	28		1		26		4				2,821
42	Tennessee	1	1	4			17	3	13	1	2	1,440	21	6			11		1	2			782
26	Texas			27	1	2	176			38	25	22	75	14	129	6	74	8	8				4,022
28	Utah			1			1					218	29	9	4	11	2		6				1,926
34	Vermont		42	123			540	1	12	10	65	418	300	92	44		23		55				2,271
36	Virginia		9	229	1		44	1	2	14	17	150	94	57	19		57	3	2	1			1,609
17	Washington	3	13	6			66	6	2	23	6	73	234	54	26	15	21	1	49	1	8		8,774
19	West Virginia		224	799			743		286	32	75	2,608	120	750	20		91	50	12		2		8,691
12	Wisconsin	2	282	228			1,800	2	10	19	29	28	72	666	2		29	9	35		2		14,689
37	Wyoming		1	1			27	9			3	4,152	71	30	3			19	3				956
55	Tourists			2			15			7		135	183		12	22	1	1	12	24	4		2,229
	Grand total	4,929	18,604	46,080	227	17	102,437	4,855	7,818	3,746	14,473	62,284	16,144	52,368	5,590	1,658	4,822	2,145	2,531	1,548	351		1,026,499

TABLE VIII.—REPORT OF ALIENS (EXCLUSIVE OF ALIENS IN TRANSIT) ADMITTED INTO THE UNITED STATES FOR THE YEAR ENDING JUNE 30, 1905, SHOWING RACE OR PEOPLE, BY OCCUPATION.

Rank	Occupation	African (black)	Armenian	Bohemian and Moravian	Bulgarian, Servian, and Montenegrin	Chinese	Croatian and Slovenian	Cuban	Dalmatian, Bosnian, and Harzegovinian	Dutch and Flemish	East India	English	Filipino	Finnish	French	German	Greek	Hebrew	Irish	Italian (north)	Italian (south)	Japanese
	PROFESSIONAL OCCUPATIONS.																					
41	Actors	2	1	4	–	10	3	20	–	11	14	446	–	–	63	189	–	25	32	58	58	44
59	Architects	1	1	3	–	–	–	3	1	8	–	178	–	4	36	148	–	21	15	10	10	3
16	Clergy	14	8	8	2	1	–	7	–	32	5	355	–	12	118	153	4	67	177	52	69	36
46	Editors	2	2	3	1	–	4	14	–	5	3	111	–	3	17	29	8	23	14	9	6	12
63	Electricians	–	–	5	1	–	2	2	–	14	–	145	–	2	19	86	8	72	37	24	20	1
19	Engineers (professional)	–	–	14	–	–	3	25	–	23	2	647	–	9	62	186	3	51	59	20	24	20
50	Lawyers (professional)	5	1	1	–	–	1	76	–	14	–	144	–	1	40	61	–	7	27	12	25	3
37	Literary and scientific persons	4	1	6	1	–	–	9	–	17	1	177	–	7	34	217	6	96	27	19	15	7
29	Musicians	4	3	33	1	3	1	7	–	22	2	196	–	8	112	327	8	242	20	38	240	1
68	Officials (government)	3	–	3	–	10	6	44	–	22	–	192	–	2	80	223	7	94	23	29	39	74
51	Physicians	5	–	9	–	–	5	99	–	18	2	193	–	9	50	190	3	94	30	34	72	21
43	Sculptors and artists	1	4	18	–	–	–	9	–	30	2	141	–	1	131	189	5	47	–	116	52	20
38	Teachers	–	2	1	1	–	5	24	–	33	–	333	–	5	365	474	3	322	146	31	45	37
73	Other professional	39	21	–	6	14	1	–	–	–	–	9	–	–	6	26	17	2	–	3	1	1
	Total	80	44	110	14	38	31	339	1	249	31	3,267	1	63	1,133	2,448	72	1,163	611	455	676	280
	SKILLED OCCUPATIONS.																					
12	Bakers	13	19	137	8	2	28	25	3	95	–	211	–	12	76	1,027	109	1,460	109	201	571	7
13	Barbers and hairdressers	31	21	25	16	2	9	34	4	16	–	96	–	1	31	390	33	578	27	82	1,718	13
14	Blacksmiths	28	33	149	19	–	75	3	–	56	–	266	–	42	43	683	44	1,568	210	168	909	2
60	Bookbinders	1	2	11	1	–	1	–	2	2	–	26	–	1	3	54	3	705	16	1	10	–
45	Brewers	1	–	20	–	–	6	10	–	7	–	33	–	2	4	246	–	32	7	9	–	–
15	Butchers	4	14	204	11	3	24	–	17	75	–	258	–	2	43	956	24	2,036	96	65	278	3
61	Cabinetmakers	1	1	3	–	–	7	–	6	7	–	118	–	3	12	79	3	1,219	17	20	26	–
1	Carpenters and joiners	106	34	301	13	3	119	21	3	166	4	1,093	–	115	96	1,529	100	5,070	399	347	1,831	2
2	Clerks and accountants	89	20	86	9	25	40	259	–	133	–	2,172	–	38	300	1,694	221	2,512	1,336	128	1,295	33
17	Dressmakers	33	10	15	–	–	9	1	–	20	–	320	–	13	214	316	–	1,589	654	161	615	84
20	Engineers (stationary) and firemen	24	12	26	3	1	11	17	5	110	–	968	–	29	314	687	7	110	275	125	96	15
47	Engravers	–	–	2	–	–	1	–	–	1	–	26	–	–	12	29	1	40	1	8	2	–

CHART 4.

BUREAU OF IMMIGRATION
F. H. SARGENT Commissioner-General

Proportion of Immigration and number of Immigrants going to each state during the fiscal year ending June 30, 1905.

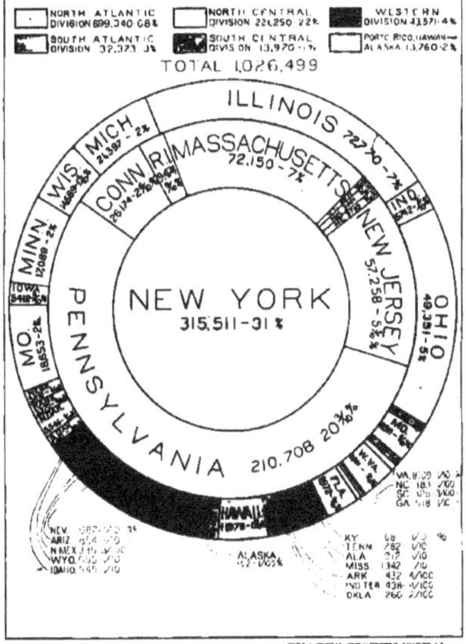

TOTAL 1,026,499

65	Furriers and fur workers			4	3		4			3		8			9	25	4	620	3	1	10	
21	Gardeners	1	2	25	25	3	5			114		272		10	47	253	13	43	99	30	165	9
66	Hat and cap makers		1	2	1				1	1		24		2	5	41	2	1,009	5	17	22	
22	Iron and steel workers		24	69	1		10	4		11		567		20	19	236	7	95	190	40	67	
49	Jewelers	2	8			1		1		3	1	49		1	23	22	3	193	8	8	22	1
23	Locksmiths		4	187	3		46		1	5		17		1	6	803	6	1,589	5	21	14	
24	Machinists	3	9	41	2		6	14		26		564		28	74	360	10	366	129	41	71	4
7	Mariners	247	2	30	6		477	14	264	119	5	752	1	411	184	597	379	52	224	292	1,832	57
25	Masons	31	11	173	12		232	5	12	41		915		18	28	717	72	469	233	1,374	3,161	3
26	Mechanics (not specified)	4	7	5	1		4	17		17		244		7	59	146	12	129	48	47	194	2
39	Metal workers (other than iron, steel, and tin)	4	13	12		3	1	1		13		212		9	18	135	17	559	51	13	86	3
27	Millers		2	42	2		15		2	13		31		1	7	225	3	211	13	23	139	2
67	Milliners	11		1			1			4		60			22	35	2	273	73	11	26	
28	Miners			251	15	2	343		12	97		2,435		131	455	713	32	15	443	1,843	492	5
30	Painters and glaziers	14	11	44	2	1	8	10		62		375		24	55	393	14	2,849	88	59	190	4
69	Photographers		6	3	3		1	3		4		46		2	12	42	1	214	3	6	22	14
52	Plasterers	2		2				2		6		163			2	11		11	76	15	16	1
53	Plumbers	4	1	1			1			6		317		1	2	22		93	83	5	9	
54	Printers	10	1	6	2		1	8		8		186		2	13	132	14	387	44	7	78	7
55	Saddlers and harness makers	7		26			12			1		48		4	7	142	2	358	37	7	34	
18	Seamstresses	116	7	133	2	6	16	1	1	24		67		34	33	349	10	2,068	235	48	677	
56	Shipwrights	4		3								22		1		1			9			
9	Shoemakers	31	163	240	17	4	91	2	6	42		165		35	42	762	129	3,824	134	287	4,004	3
31	Stonecutters		4	26			15		2	4		143		12	7	102	6	32	71	409	567	1
10	Tailors	57	83	273	29	10	73	8	6	40		248		101	58	906	79	22,334	177	239	2,591	36
32	Tanners and curriers		1	19	6		20			6		31		9	6	89	14	531	20	15	28	
70	Textile workers (not specified)	6	4	1	1		2	2		5		190		1	11	74	1	148	73	9	21	2
34	Tinners	1	7	32		1	3		1	4		44		4	14	215	5	1,016	12	10	63	
35	Tobacco workers	489	7	7		5	1	1,918		166		47		2	6	58	31	651	7	8	23	1
71	Upholsterers	1		4	1				1	10		49		2	2	55		258	7	4	9	
57	Watch and clock makers	3	1	6			1	3		5		53		7	45	80	3	667	6	7	38	5
36	Weavers and spinners		44	54			7			89		1,519		6	167	437	10	815	368	169	152	12
58	Wheelwrights	2		27	3		13			3		34			3	176	1	74	4	6	4	
72	Woodworkers (not specified)	7		37	2	1	7	1		11		80		3	21	194	8	283	65	19	90	1
74	Other skilled	8	3	61	2	2	7	5	2	47		626		1	100	357	23	985	172	81	143	25
	Total	1,396	592	2,826	221	75	1,752	2,389	351	1,698	10	16,170	2	1,148	2,710	16,595	1,524	60,135	6,362	6,486	21,411	358
	MISCELLANEOUS OCCUPATIONS.																					
42	Agents	1		1		1		4		21		381		4	47	48	2	31	51	20	9	7
44	Bankers		2					13		29		215			35	61	1	5	6	4	8	14
62	Draymen, hackmen, and teamsters	6		25			4	3	1	10		107			30	54		61	95	60	232	2
4	Farm laborers	43	115	480	1,301	28	4,818	6	860	820	2	612		1,759	410	5,650	2,639	498	1,925	6,181	60,529	5,883
3	Farmers	46	58	409	195	31	796	30	62	655		760		57	242	2,206	414	122	982	1,397	4,814	380
64	Fishermen	12				1	3		10	5		20		7		17	7	20	58	13	332	20
48	Hotel keepers	5	1	3	1	3	2	23		4		96			29	105	17	24	52	29	12	60

TABLE VIII.—REPORT OF ALIENS (EXCLUSIVE OF ALIENS IN TRANSIT) ADMITTED INTO THE UNITED STATES FOR THE YEAR ENDING JUNE 30, 1905, SHOWING RACE OR PEOPLE, BY OCCUPATION—Continued.

Rank	Occupation	African (black)	Armenian	Bohemian and Moravian	Bulgarian, Servian, and Montenegrin	Chinese	Croatian and Slovenian	Cuban	Dalmatian, Bosnian, and Herzegovinian	Dutch and Flemish	East India	English	Filipino	Finnish	French	German	Greek	Hebrew	Irish	Italian (north)	Italian (south)	Japanese
	MISCELLANEOUS OCCUPATIONS—continued.																					
5	Laborers	411	239	1,437	3,746	287	22,138	77	1,153	818	35	2,825		8,122	445	11,992	5,818	8,159	13,197	14,291	56,040	743
38	Manufacturers	3		21			2	19	1	16		524			101	211	9	90	56	14	32	28
6	Merchants and dealers	51	75	84	17	1,149	31	561	7	250	34	1,986	1	14	653	3,335	367	4,596	435	557	1,415	777
8	Servants	722	214	2,006	52	160	2,408	511	66	450	7	4,477		3,043	1,479	12,679	387	8,000	23,224	2,752	8,669	207
75	Other miscellaneous	14	2	8	3	4	3	35	1	57	3	735		4	102	238	18	135	442	39	96	50
	Total	1,314	706	4,474	5,315	1,664	30,205	1,282	2,161	3,185	81	12,738	1	13,010	3,573	36,596	9,679	21,741	40,523	25,357	132,188	8,171
11	No occupation (including all children under 14 years of age)	808	586	4,347	273	194	3,116	3,249	126	3,416	23	18,690	2	2,791	3,931	26,721	869	46,871	6,770	7,632	32,115	2,212
	Grand total	3,598	1,878	11,757	5,823	1,971	35,104	7,259	2,639	8,498	145	50,865	5	17,012	11,347	82,360	12,144	129,910	54,266	39,930	186,390	11,021

TABLE VIII.—REPORT OF ALIENS (EXCLUSIVE OF ALIENS IN TRANSIT) ADMITTED INTO THE UNITED STATES FOR THE YEAR ENDING JUNE 30, 1905, SHOWING RACE OF PEOPLE, BY OCCUPATION—Continued.

Rank	Occupation	Korean	Lithuanian	Magyar	Mexican	Pacific Islander	Polish	Portuguese	Roumanian	Russian	Ruthenian or Russniak	Scandinavian (Norwegians, Danes, and Swedes)	Scotch	Slovak	Spanish	Spanish-American	Syrian	Turkish	Welsh	West Indian (except Cuban)	All other peoples	Total aliens
	PROFESSIONAL OCCUPATIONS.																					
41	Actors		2	16	1		2		2	23		27	49		33	6	1	1	1	15		1,157
59	Architects		3	12			2	5	1	3		28	41		5	2				1	9	545
16	Clergy			29			30	2	1	12		81	65		45	7	16	1	24	7		1,459
46	Editors			11			13	1		5	4	9	16		5	10			3	1		326
63	Electricians			9						3		82	22		26		2		2	2		572
19	Engineers (professional)		1	14			14	4	1	6		181	136		23			1	17	10		1,583
50	Lawyers			16			1	2		2		17	24						4	7		566
37	Literary and scientific persons	1	2	6			8	1	1	14		35	40		2	17			4	2		769
29	Musicians		3	27	2		49	2	2	4		31	16	1	8	39			4	1	3	1,525
68	Officials (government)	1		39	1	1	6	7	2	13	1	34	18	9	28	6	3	3	9	9	2	966
51	Physicians			14	3		2	5	1	15		64	35		28	44	2	1	8	10	3	1,043
43	Sculptors and artists			13	3		14	1	2	14		14	17	4	15	29		4	1	1		819
33	Teachers		2	27	1	1	18	1	1	18		103	62	3	11	6	20	2	12	26	3	2,256
73	Other professional			1			1			1		1				9			1			57
	Total	2	13	234	18	2	160	31	14	133	7	707	541	19	224	175	47	14	78	92	17	13,643
	SKILLED OCCUPATIONS.																					
12	Bakers		12	52	1		173	4	10	18	3	232	128	19	48	1	6	17	5	4		4,845
13	Barbers and hairdressers		8	53			41	12	11	5		41	20	5	8	2	17	12	4	4	8	3,366
14	Blacksmiths		45	281			417	8	13	26	20	520	132	134	13		22	6	18	11	7	5,964
60	Bookbinders		2	10			16		1	4		35	12	3							1	920
45	Brewers			2			6					21	5	44								408
15	Butchers		45	180			218		10	8	4	132	61	1		4	14	4	1	4		4,759
61	Cabinetmakers		139	15			96	2	6	5	1	70	42		11		1		7	1		1,806
1	Carpenters and joiners	4	13	353	8		698	26	23	60	26	1,684	641	197	64	50	99	15	39	32		15,496
2	Clerks and accountants		3	113			100	26	12	32	2	918	575	19	399	1	58	21	55	123	7	11,986
17	Dressmakers			70			78	11	10	8	4	226	101	6	8		26	3	23	20	1	4,575
20	Engineers (stationary) and firemen		21	50	5		39	42	8	33	2	576	373	20	549	27	1		40	18	3	4,709
47	Engravers											9	8	2	4	1		2				146

TABLE VIII.—REPORT OF ALIENS (EXCLUSIVE OF ALIENS IN TRANSIT) ADMITTED INTO THE UNITED STATES FOR THE YEAR ENDING JUNE 30, 1905, SHOWING RACE OR PEOPLE, BY OCCUPATION—Continued.

Rank	Occupation	Korean	Lithuanian	Magyar	Mexican	Pacific Islander	Polish	Portuguese	Roumanian	Russian	Ruthenian or Russniak	Scandinavian (Norwegians, Danes, and Swedes)	Scotch	Slovak	Spanish	Spanish-American	Syrian	Turkish	Welsh	West Indian (except Cuban)	All other peoples	Total aliens
	MISCELLANEOUS OCCUPATIONS—continued.																					
65	Furriers and fur workers			17			15	2	2	2	1	9	2	9	1	1		4	1	2		756
21	Gardeners		9	29			58		3	3		137	99	11	4		2	3	6	2	36	1,473
66	Hat and cap makers		7	10			15	1	1	3	9	164		10	36		2	1		96	4	1,190
22	Iron and steel workers		78	45	24	8	68	1	4	2	2	11	233	54	11	4	3		28	5		2,071
49	Jewelers		21	7	3		1		12	26		14	1	80	230	47						857
23	Locksmiths		8	170			280	1	6	14	9	299	182	10	40	1	12	3	20	2		3,319
24	Machinists		20	64			49	1	5	72	2	4,431	180	8	15	2	51	12	24	96	36	2,420
7	Mariners		21	10			14	52	7	6	8	291	757	120			81	2	26	5	4	11,220
25	Masons		2	129			221	9	4	4	5	144	64	5	7	1	4	1	4	2		9,212
26	Mechanics (not specified)			15			20		1		3	62	55	33	1	2	3		13	1	1	1,230
39	Metal workers (other than iron, steel, and tin)						19		1	1		64	18	5	1				3	9		1,345
27	Millers		3	12			68		5	4		28	12	33	32	3		5	1	1		988
67	Milliners			57			1	3	2		30	212		259	5	3	4	2	481	6		567
28	Miners		434	164			386	3	1	1	3	373	1,036	24	1	1	5	1	6	2		10,360
30	Painters and glaziers		7	42	1		90	1	5	20		56	134		4		3	2	8	1	1	4,928
69	Photographers			3			6	2	2	20	1	5	14	2	3		2		12			477
52	Plasterers			3			4			3	1	22	347		3	1			2			677
53	Plumbers			4			15		1		4	64	135	2	2		2	2			1	729
54	Printers		1	34				1	1	1		43	55	34	7		21		2		1	1,095
55	Saddlers and harness makers			24	1		62		4	4	1	343	19	11	2				1	1		888
18	Seamstresses		5	69			140	12	1	5	4	6	21	288	12		116	18	20	54	2	4,530
56	Shipwrights		13								33	265	17	7	67			5	16	1		67
9	Shoemakers		75	327	2		673	13	10	30		161	45	134	18	2	80	20	1	12		11,899
31	Stonecutters		3	11			15	5	1	137	32	370	395	82	1	1	9	3		15		2,101
10	Tailors		178	219	41		589	3	30		2	38	71	1	1		3		1	1	2	29,266
32	Tanners and curriers		3	35	4		31		5	3		15	12	22	4	1	4		20		4	1,021
70	Textile workers (not specified)		1	2			1	1	1	1	1	50	40	3	403		5		16	1		618
34	Tinners		1	41			42			3		35	15		1				1	1	1	1,634
35	Tobacco workers		2	4	2		3		1	2	1		4						15	1	1	3,892

Code	Occupation	Total
71	Upholsterers	465
57	Watch and clock makers	1,017
36	Weavers and spinners	4,439
58	Wheelwrights	480
72	Woodworkers (not specified)	1,143
74	Other skilled	3,228
	Total	180,112
	MISCELLANEOUS OCCUPATIONS.	
42	Agents	773
44	Bankers	465
62	Draymen, hackmen, and teamsters	819
4	Farm laborers	142,187
3	Farmers	18,474
64	Fishermen	1,086
48	Hotel keepers	538
6	Laborers	297,450
38	Manufacturers	1,399
6	Merchants and dealers	19,579
8	Servants	125,473
75	Other miscellaneous	2,483
	Total	600,726
11	No occupation (including all children under 14 years of age)	232,018
	Grand total	1,026,499

TABLE IX.—REPORT OF ALIENS (EXCLUSIVE OF ALIENS IN TRANSIT) ADMITTED INTO THE UNITED STATES FOR THE YEAR ENDING JUNE 30, 1905, SHOWING DESTINATION BY OCCUPATION.

Rank	Occupation	Alabama	Alaska	Arizona	Arkansas	California	Colorado	Connecticut	Delaware	District of Columbia	Florida	Georgia	Hawaii	Idaho	Illinois	Indian Ter.	Indiana	Iowa	Kansas	Kentucky
	PROFESSIONAL OCCUPATIONS.																			
41	Actors	1		4		93	2	4		4	33	1	3	1	54		1	2	1	
50	Architects	6			3	20	2	5		13	8		2		27		1	1		
16	Clergy	1	1	5	5	55	4	26		3	20	3	16	2	90	2	1	18	15	6
46	Editors			1		15	2	4		1	3		4		12				1	
63	Electricians		1	1		13	1	10		11	1	4			37		7		1	
19	Engineers (professional)	7		15		97	2	12	1	12	11		2	3	60		1	8		
50	Lawyers	3		1	2	30	1		1	7	13	1	2		8		2	1	3	2
37	Literary and scientific persons	2		2		33	2		2	6	1	1	2		32		4			
29	Musicians		1			29	2	4		77	5				75		1			1
68	Officials (government)	5				49	2	13		9	14		11		16		2			
51	Physicians	1	1			56		4		1	26	2	8		43		2	3	1	1
43	Sculptors and artists					29		8	1						32					
33	Teachers	4				97	1	11					2		105		1	4		4
73	Other professional	1		2	2	7	8	43	2	30	9	7	3	1	2		9	10	2	
	Total	31	4	31	12	623	37	144	6	174	189	19	55	7	593	2	29	42	24	14
	SKILLED OCCUPATIONS.																			
12	Bakers	1		3	3	90	7	85	4	8	41	2	5	3	352		22	25	11	9
13	Barbers and hairdressers	3	3	1		28	1	84	3	12	60	2	5		117		9	2	2	2
14	Blacksmiths	7	1	5	2	64	27	120	2	7	8	3	1	4	456	3	44	48	18	8
60	Bookbinders					3	3	9							48		2	3		2
45	Brewers	3		1		17		4		5	1				40		3	3	1	1
15	Butchers	1		1	1	42	6	90	2	6	22	1	2	3	437		27	28	7	1
61	Cabinetmakers					14		37	5	2	2		1		96		4	3	3	1
1	Carpenters and joiners	19	1	8	3	270	40	826	8	13	98	3	13	3	1,065		52	85	35	10
2	Clerks and accountants	25	2	22	7	379	37	173	15	49	465	8	28	17	772	4	40	85	22	5
17	Dressmakers	6		1	2	96	12	108	10	18	9	16	4	13	231	2	11	16	7	18
20	Engineers (stationary) and firemen	26		5	2	164	21	44	3	137	26	1	5	3	159		9	15	10	5
47	Engravers				2	3		5	1			1			12			1		2
65	Furriers and fur workers					2	6	10		2	9				32			1		1
21	Gardeners	5	1		2	85	6	32		2	9	1		4	113		1	8	4	1
66	Hat and cap makers	1				3	1	18	1	3	4	1		1	41		16			1

	Occupation																			Total
22	Iron and steel workers	2	9	3	17		136	2			8	3		63	5	41		5		3	
49	Jewelers		3	2	17		14		1	1	1	6		4	1	9		1	1		
28	Locksmiths		3	7	14		270	1		2	2	8	2	65	4	16		1	7	10	
24	Machinists	7	18	10	8	5	146	1	10	22	12	6	11	42	11	49	8	2	1	124	
7	Mariners	1	4	17	35		271	1	1	1	329	25	1	114	21	1,381	1	5	1	4	
25	Masons	25	2	34	8		523	9			29	3		261	33	191	45	23		1	
26	Mechanics (not specified)	6	2	4	8		116	5			4	1		27	4	21		1			
39	Metal workers (other than iron, steel, and tin)		2	6	6		56	1	2	2	2	1	1	44	1	20	1	2	1	1	
27	Millers	1	2	9	8		108		2	3	3	12	2	24	308	14		5	26	20	
67	Milliners		1	3	256		26	38	4	1	2	6	4	81	6	6	45	23	2	26	
28	Miners	2	332	138	15	64	1,162		5	5	13	1	3	98		255		220		1	
30	Painters and glaziers	2		28	1		231	2	6	7	4	4	2	6	4	51		2	1	1	
69	Photographers		2	2			25		1	3	2	1	4	13	5	17		1		2	
52	Plasterers	5	1	9	3	1	25			13	9	1		30	1	21				4	
53	Plumbers	6		7	5		39		1	1	3	2	3	15	1	25		1		6	
54	Printers	23	6	30	15		64		2	4	55	7		119	21	28	1	1		7	
55	Saddlers and harnessmakers	1			1		75		6	1	27	46		317	9	13		3		2	
18	Seamstresses		15	40	31	1	329	2	1	5	1	6	21	47	17	51		3		3	
66	Shipwrights		3	6	12		1	6	7	7	29	64	15	448	2	9		1		1	
9	Shoemakers	1	12	63	45		628		1	3	5	3	1	15	2	82	2	1		1	
31	Stonecutters	2		3			66	2		13	2	1		9	3	24		1		2	
10	Tailors	2	1	1	2	1	1,275		1	1	2,790	2		32	1	147	1	5	2	4	
32	Tanners and curriers	1	2	4	8		110		1	1	4	1		12	1	9				1	
70	Textile workers (not specified)			3	1	1		2		4	2	1	2	32	6	7					
34	Tinners		1		2		19			1	3	1		9	2	12				67	
35	Tobacco workers	1	2	8	8		77		1	1	3	2		32	3	36		3	2		
71	Upholsterers	2	1	3	3		33		1	4	3	2	1	170	1	2	1	3	1		
57	Watch and clock makers	1	6	8	7		18			1	42	1		8	6	8		1			
36	Weavers and spinners	2	8	8	10		50	2	1	1	320	1		22	2	19		1		4	
58	Wheelwrights	2	3	10	5	1	120				38	1		67	1	68	2	5		1	
72	Woodworkers (not specified)	1			4		53			5	197	4			8						
74	Other skilled				28	1	184		2			5								67	
	Total	**156**	**562**	**785**	**811**	**83**	**10,304**	**121**	**109**	**113**	**4,094**	**481**	**131**	**3,351**	**644**	**3,910**	**85**	**326**	**46**	**299**	

MISCELLANEOUS OCCUPATIONS.

42	Agents		3	1	2	1	40	1	3	3	10	2		3	5	33	1	1	17	4
44	Bankers			1	2		8		1		7	2		1	2	22		1	2	2
62	Draymen, hackmen, and teamsters	1	4	8			62				8	4	1	19	2	22			1	
4	Farm laborers	50	230	523	1,046	48	7,849	64	9,949	31	156	300	209	3,592	664	1,919	27	67		32
3	Farmers	15	165	390	197	4	1,539	80	101	8	65	24	15	469	238	898	14	27		16
64	Fishermen		2	5	1		43	3	3		23			8	2	36				
48	Hotel keepers		2	1		127	30	129	5	70	42	3			1	43	64	228	46	99
5	Laborers	73	602	1,129	2,444		22,861	12	97	39	320	406	482	8,018	1,328	3,910	1	1	1	2
38	Manufacturers	1	5	4	1		51		130		38	5	2	12	4	49	10	28	3	67
6	Merchants and dealers	29	25	54	51		766				197	55	7	181	35	1,504				

TABLE IX.—REPORT OF ALIENS (EXCLUSIVE OF ALIENS IN TRANSIT) ADMITTED INTO THE UNITED STATES FOR THE YEAR ENDING JUNE 30, 1905, SHOWING DESTINATION, BY OCCUPATION—Continued.

Rank.	Occupation.	Alabama.	Alaska.	Arizona.	Arkansas.	California.	Colorado.	Connecticut.	Delaware.	District of Columbia.	Florida.	Georgia.	Hawaii.	Idaho.	Illinois.	Indian Territory.	Indiana.	Iowa.	Kansas.	Kentucky.
	MISCELLANEOUS OCCUPATIONS—continued.																			
8	Servants	58	11	30	35	2,025	419	4,402	170	240	943	43	68	61	10,830	35	528	853	291	78
75	Other miscellaneous	11	1	4	1	117	16	38	2	74	22	2	15	7	117		16	21	6	6
	Total	290	81	387	153	10,578	2,715	16,750	888	1,115	1,831	196	10,377	357	44,196	215	4,290	2,990	1,335	253
11	No occupation (including all children under 14 years of age)	302	21	110	182	5,712	1,095	5,929	206	560	2,908	190	1,487	160	17,677	138	1,612	1,595	1,449	258
	Grand total	912	152	854	432	20,823	4,491	26,174	1,231	2,330	8,972	518	11,978	645	72,770	438	6,742	5,412	3,370	661

Rank.	Occupation.	Louisiana.	Maine.	Maryland.	Massachusetts.	Michigan.	Minnesota.	Mississippi.	Missouri.	Montana.	Nebraska.	Nevada.	New Hampshire.	New Jersey.	New Mexico.	New York.	North Carolina.	North Dakota.	Ohio.	Oklahoma.
	PROFESSIONAL OCCUPATIONS.																			
41	Actors	6	1	1	22		8		44	3	4			20		688		7	9	
59	Architects		4	2	28		5		43		3			41		238			16	1
16	Clergy	30	12	17	86	10	33	2	51	2	13	1	3	42	7	477	1	10	82	1
46	Editors	5		1	11	30	3		33		2	1		6		165	1	2	4	
63	Electricians	3	2	4	54	8	7		117		2		2	30		273	1	2	9	
19	Engineers (professional)	35		8	76	8	15		87	6		1	3	42	2	598	1	1	21	
50	Lawyers	9	1	6	9	25	2		65	1	1			5		304	1	1	1	
37	Literary and scientific persons	5	2	1	35	1	6		60	2	7	1	4	58	2	369	1	1	11	1
29	Musicians	23		17	74	10	4	1	160	1		2		48		777	1		30	
58	Officials (Government)		1	19	19	13	4		244		1		1	5	2	340	1		1	
51	Physicians	14		3	50	3	11		100	1			1	20	1	484			8	
43	Sculptors and artists	6		8	37	4	3		28		1		1	17		535		4	17	1

	17	3	32	197	22	18	1	186 3	3	7	2	10	87 4	3	965 34	6	10	1
Teachers																		
Other professional																		
Total	170	26	125	698	129	119	4	1,175	19	42	8	24	405	15	6,267	12	40	202
SKILLED OCCUPATIONS.																		
Bakers	25	11	56	311	66	61	3	93	8	21	2	12	250	1	2,405		14	118
Barbers and hairdressers	25	3	41	219	26	11	3	42	1	7		3	190	3	1,871	2	9	102
Blacksmiths	12	14	81	414	122	106	4	85	6	31		9	322		2,278		35	293
Bookbinders	3	2	18	63	7	9		6	1	1			29		575	2	2	13
Brewers			5	16	7	6		27	3	3	1	1	21	1	156			15
Butchers	10	12	92	283	82	53	3	80	10	28		4	277		2,232		7	167
Cabinetmakers	2	6	27	184	32	26		20		1			66		951		3	28
Carpenters and joiners	51	36	238	972	295	308	10	231	30	73	11	17	828	2	6,973	6	110	566
Clerks and accountants	91	31	76	885	130	216	11	246	24	46	7	35	512	1	5,568	2	47	198
Dressmakers	13	12	27	426	30	40	1	44	2	15	1	4	219	2	2,375	1	9	93
Engineers (stationary) and firemen	58	15	43	243	60	36	1	359	12	11		5	171	1	2,269	5	10	99
Engravers			2	8	3	2		2					9		76			1
Furriers and fur workers		4	7	36	1	4		5	4				23		534			9
Gardeners	14	1	11	139	47	20	1	56		12		6	95		454	2	5	63
Hat and cap makers		25	18	75	9	6		19	1	2			44		763			30
Iron and steel workers	5		16	236	35	25	1	42	6	6		7	121		547		8	117
Jewelers	1	2	3	12	1	3		8	1				22	1	230	1	1	6
Locksmiths	1	5	62	122	38	17	1	54	2	12		8	199		1,545		3	185
Machinists	2	46	47	250	74	36	36	37	10	9	3	8	132	3	888	1	9	91
Mariners	547	26	105	616	77	62	62	55	31	9	4	8	389	1	5,232	2	22	85
Masons	39	2	139	470	165	90	114	210	2	23		38	502	2	3,768	2	18	291
Mechanics (not specified)	2		6	86	18	24	6	16		2		1	78		558		5	26
Metal workers (other than iron, steel, and tin)	2	3	11	83	15	8		15		2	1	4	77		681		3	26
Millers	5	2	11	46	11	25		29	1	10	1	1	57	1	306		10	51
Milliners		1	4	66	2	5		6	1				26		299	3		9
Miners	8	26	60	214	634	124	13	145	42	18	16	8	147	28	2,811		30	533
Painters and glaziers	9	10	66	385	52	64		56	6	15		11	227	2	256		23	84
Photographers	3	1	8	28	5	8		11	1				15		398		1	8
Plasterers			2	48	9	6		10				2	36		257			12
Plumbers	1	9	13	65	5	14		3	1			4	59		586	2	2	17
Printers	2	3	13	74	15	16		26	1	3		3	41		376	3	9	20
Saddlers and harnessmakers	8	2	62	64	12	14		14	7	4	2	2	50		487	1	4	25
Seamstresses		2	1	314	21	49	3	45	2	17		6	245	1	2,487		10	91
Shipwrights		24	175	1,064	34	1		147	1		1		3		32			
Shoemakers	72	47	29	287	152	77	10	11	1	40	1	31	698	1	5,485	1	27	412
Stonecutters	1	63	586	2,240	23	31	1	278	42	3	2	17	79		701	4	6	59
Tailors	33		12	72	140	137	6	2	6	30	1	28	1,008		18,391		27	496
Tanners and curriers	8	7	1	90	13	12	1	31	1	5			75		243		1	32
Textile workers (not specified)	2	6	3	101	5	2	1	8		4			52		868		2	14
Tinners	1	1	30	237	18	12		4				5	73		558		1	50
Tobacco workers	3		15	34	7	5		17				1	37		284		2	15
Upholsterers	5		4	71	8	6		4		3		1	17		594		2	10
Watch and clock makers			11		5	10	1						36				2	10

TABLE IX.—REPORT OF ALIENS (EXCLUSIVE OF ALIENS IN TRANSIT) ADMITTED INTO THE UNITED STATES FOR THE YEAR ENDING JUNE 30, 1905, SHOWING DESTINATION, BY OCCUPATION—Continued.

Rank	Occupation	Louisiana	Maine	Maryland	Massachusetts	Michigan	Minnesota	Mississippi	Missouri	Montana	Nebraska	Nevada	New Hampshire	New Jersey	New Mexico	New York	North Carolina	North Dakota	Ohio	Oklahoma
	SKILLED OCCUPATIONS—cont'd.																			
36	Weavers and spinners	6	67	15	1,212	34	20	1	23	4	14		51	528		1,037	1	4	48	1
58	Wheelwrights			9	20	14	7		11		3		1	31		125		6	49	
72	Wood workers (not specified)	3	3	17	84	10	12		28	2				73	1	502	1	1	48	
74	Other skilled	6	23	38	254	34	12	2	45	4	10	1	8	262		1,398		4	124	1
	Total	1,081	556	2,328	13,234	2,601	1,884	198	2,710	332	497	58	350	8,451	52	82,249	39	493	4,889	35
	MISCELLANEOUS OCCUPATIONS.																			
42	Agents	12	3	2	79	5	9	3	24	1	1		1	27		348	4	2	6	
44	Bankers	8	1		11		2		23	1				4		294			4	
62	Draymen, hackmen, and teamsters	11	4	3	77	11	8	202	19	1	4	2		34	37	313	5	4	22	
4	Farm laborers	290	282	442	6,214	2,688	1,705	18	2,434	279	257	163	288	9,190	16	32,910	2	812	9,541	13
3	Farmers	132	24	69	786	519	480	3	434	179	208	93	27	709		3,609	1	292	1,003	26
64	Fishermen	18	3	3	116	47	53		31	1		1		21		366		33	7	
48	Hotel keepers	5	1	4	28	2	6		15	2	2			17		194		1	19	
5	Laborers	995	893	2,022	20,324	7,934	5,761	220	4,979	613	669	240	1,216	16,212	88	62,259	28	1,267	18,251	20
38	Manufacturers			6	57	17		1	158	4		1	1	58	1	639	1	1	19	
8	Merchants and dealers	236	39	156	803	104	96	21	1,236	25	36	6	19	552	7	10,152	5	20	238	3
6	Servants	348	306	905	13,834	2,100	2,762	78	1,313	246	460	42	581	9,299	15	41,021	9	835	4,577	21
75	Other miscellaneous	16	7	26	88	23	19	1	121	20	7	3	6	104	2	1,068	2	3	34	
	Total	2,076	1,563	3,638	42,417	18,450	10,907	547	10,792	1,371	1,644	551	2,088	36,222	166	158,173	57	3,270	33,706	83
11	No occupation (including all children under 14 years of age)	1,774	648	2,420	15,802	5,217	4,229	598	3,976	403	1,227	70	539	12,180	102	73,821	75	1,743	10,604	138
	Grand total	5,101	2,798	8,511	72,151	21,397	17,089	1,342	18,653	2,125	3,410	687	3,001	57,258	335	315,510	188	5,546	49,351	260

TABLE IX.—REPORT OF ALIENS (EXCLUSIVE OF ALIENS IN TRANSIT) ADMITTED INTO THE UNITED STATES FOR THE YEAR ENDING JUNE 30, 1905, SHOWING DESTINATION, BY OCCUPATION—Continued.

Rank	Occupation	Oregon	Pennsylvania	Philippine Islands	Porto Rico	Rhode Island	South Carolina	South Dakota	Tennessee	Texas	Utah	Vermont	Virginia	Washington	West Virginia	Wisconsin	Wyoming	Tourist	Total aliens
	PROFESSIONAL OCCUPATIONS.																		
41	Actors	2	39		12	1				16		2		45	1	8		20	1,157
59	Architects	12	50		1	6			1	4		1	4	2	1	3	1	8	545
16	Clergy	3	115		34	9	2		2	25	2	4	7	17	4	19		48	1,459
46	Editors	2	11		1	3				3			1	3		7		17	326
63	Electricians	3	60			5	4			8	11		1	7		2	1	5	572
19	Engineers (professional)	1	129		23	13		8	2	2	4	1	18	36	5	7		104	1,563
50	Lawyers	2	9		2	7			1	3		3	2	8	5	7		35	566
37	Literary and scientific persons	1	43		2	1		3	2	8	1	3	2	6	2	2		25	769
29	Musicians	2	129		13	5	26	2	1	5	4	2	2	5	5	6	2	66	1,525
68	Officials (Government)	6	19		23	4		2	1	5			2	12	12	19	8	78	966
51	Physicians		74		2	10	2		1	10	3	8	3	5	2	3	3	41	1,043
43	Sculptors and artists	1	38		2	4				13	1	2	11	7	1	5		8	819
33	Teachers	2	160		9	19		3	3	13	5			2	1	10	1	41	2,256
73	Other professional		4																57
	Total	36	880		129	86	7	19	13	128	31	24	53	155	15	96	5	496	13,643
	SKILLED OCCUPATIONS.																		
12	Bakers	7	488		10	39	2	6	3	22	12	1	3	34	14	71		49	4,845
13	Barbers and hairdressers	3	355		2	49	1	14	3	9	3	11	1	4	4	21		1	5,366
14	Blacksmiths	10	976		3	36		14	3	19	13	18	8	71	30	117	3		5,964
60	Bookbinders		100			8		3						1	1	3			920
45	Brewers	2	36		2	2	4		4	2	2		2	4		11		2	408
15	Butchers	10	551			30	26	1	1	19	3	3	6	25	8	57	6	1	4,759
61	Cabinetmakers	2	219		15	17	8	8	12	57	5	11	7	13	1	17	8	4	1,806
1	Carpenters and joiners	29	1,846		142	108	2	41	13	102	26	17	33	158	52	247	8	59	15,496
2	Clerks and accountants	22	892		1	96		23	6		43	15	17	121	12	112	3	4	11,986
17	Dressmakers	6	533			71	2	5			31	5	3	18	3	27	3		4,575
20	Engineers (stationary) and firemen	6	362		8	42	21	4	2	18	8	7	63	41	7	33	4	49	4,709
47	Engravers		12		1	3				1			1	2	1	10			146
65	Furriers and fur workers	1	69			4	4		1	1	5	1	7	11	1	21	2		756
21	Gardeners	5	153		2	15	5	5	2	12		3	3		3	6			1,473
66	Hat and cap makers		127	2		8				1		1							1,190
22	Iron and steel workers	3	410		1	62	5	1	2	6	13	3	13	12	13	29		3	2,071

TABLE IX.—REPORT OF ALIENS (EXCLUSIVE OF ALIENS IN TRANSIT) ADMITTED INTO THE UNITED STATES FOR THE YEAR ENDING JUNE 30, 1905, SHOWING DESTINATION, BY OCCUPATION—Continued.

Rank	Occupation	Oregon	Pennsylvania	Philippine Islands	Porto Rico	Rhode Island	South Carolina	South Dakota	Tennessee	Texas	Utah	Vermont	Virginia	Washington	West Virginia	Wisconsin	Wyoming	Tourist	Total aliens
	SKILLED OCCUPATIONS—cont'd.																		
49	Jewelers	1	22			14	1	4	1	17	1	2	4	5		1		2	387
23	Locksmiths	10	572		2	13	1	4		17	4	8	13	30	8	42	1	1	3,319
24	Machinists	7	296		15	63	2	3	2	24	12	3	31	490	7	34		4	2,420
7	Mariners	7	526		9	80		16	3	82	2	40	6	54	22	99		9	11,220
25	Masons	2	1,734		7	56	2	8	3	41	18	1	5	10	84	105	4	1	9,212
26	Mechanics (not specified)		113			27	3	1	3	6	7				1	17	9	4	1,230
39	Metal workers (other than iron, steel, and tin)	1	177		6	27		3		16	1	1	5			12	1		1,345
27	Millers	2	163			8	1	2	1	7	4			6	4	40		2	988
67	Milliners	1	64			18	1	1		2				11	11	2	1		567
28	Miners	21	3,293			31	1	52	12	73	155	36	12	344	212	86	2	6	10,360
30	Painters and glaziers	9	442		1	44	3	13	3	15	2	3	12	19	5	56	45	1	4,928
69	Photographers	4	33			4	6	2		2	4			3		4			477
52	Plasterers	1	55		3	11		1		1	2			6		3			729
63	Plumbers	1	98			23	3	1	1	2	2	1	4	9	2	3		4	1,065
54	Printers	1	102		1	13	6	2		5	5	2	3	5		14	1	2	888
55	Saddlers and harnessmakers		129		2	6		1	1	2		4		4		19		1	
18	Seamstresses	5	364		9	35		6		13	15		2	12	2	48			4,580
56	Shipwrights		5										1		5		1		67
9	Shoemakers	9	1,774		11	126	2	14	15	33	15	237		29	58	116		1	11,899
31	Stonecutters	2	284			24	3	6	2	2	3	11	14	6	23	18	1		2,101
10	Tailors	9	3,067		5	170	6	12	19	45	13			59	25	148		2	29,266
32	Tanners and curriers	1	115		1	8		1					34		1	32		1	1,021
70	Textile workers (not specified)						1												618
34	Tinners	1	85		5	32	1	2	1	3	2	1		5	4	11		2	1,634
35	Tobacco workers		229		1	12		2	1	1	1	3	1	3		16			3,892
71	Upholsterers	1	118			5		1		1	1	1	4	3	1	8	1	4	465
57	Watch and clock makers	3	40		2	2	2		1	2			4			9	1		1,017
36	Weavers and spinners	2	94			12		4		13	22	7		8	6	7			4,439
68	Wheelwrights		501			393		2		3	5	1	3	6	1	31		1	480
72	Wood workers (not specified)	1	85		4	3	1	2		5	1			3	5	19	1	8	1,143
74	Other skilled	5	394		9	61	4	1	2	15	8	7	5	26	17	47	2	7	3,228
	Total	283	22,254	2	281	1,907	126	288	124	709	473	464	379	1,882	654	1,844	99	195	180,112

No.	MISCELLANEOUS OCCUPATIONS.																		Total
42	Agents	1	49	1	24	8			2	18	2		1	12		1		21	773
44	Bankers		4		3					64	1		1	8			1	34	465
62	Draymen, hackmen, and teamsters	2	111			13	2	4		1	4			13		10	1		819
4	Farm laborers	169	40,538		42	948	1	340	95	75	163	270	2	454	6	1,591	114	4	142,187
3	Farmers	167	3,581		93	84	17	197	19	277	54	22	186	289	2,651	463	33	35	18,474
64	Fishermen	29	27			5	5	8	4	4	1	2	32	59	230	127			1,066
48	Hotel keepers	12	34		3	7		1						36		3		9	538
5	Laborers	421	83,586	2	58	2,048	29	606	184	883	429	792	338	3,434	3,465	4,396	350	17	287,450
38	Manufacturers	5	75		5	7			1	3	2	1	2	19	2	15	2	111	1,399
6	Merchants and dealers	113	1,121		355	88	20	13	40	216	19	18	32	217	22	85		270	19,579
8	Servants	225	19,349	1	76	1,582	23	444	51	308	175	221	111	786	370	1,774	102	56	125,473
75	Other miscellaneous	10	200		32	17	2	6	2	37	4	5	13	47	4	25	8	43	2,483
	Total	1,154	148,675	4	691	4,807	99	1,619	399	1,886	857	1,331	718	5,374	6,750	8,490	614	600	600,726
11	No occupation (including all children under 14 years of age)	482	38,899		529	2,674	96	895	246	1,349	565	452	459	1,563	1,272	4,259	238	938	232,018
	Grand total	1,955	210,708	6	1,630	9,474	328	2,821	782	4,022	1,926	2,271	1,609	8,774	8,691	14,689	956	2,229	1,026,499

Table X gives the arrivals in the United States from the foreign countries whence they respectively came, of all aliens during each year since 1857 arranged in the form of reports of alien passengers issued prior to the organization of the Bureau:

TABLE X.—NUMBER AND NATIONALITIES OF IMMIGRANTS ARRIVED IN THE UNITED STATES FROM 1857 TO 1905, INCLUSIVE.

Country.	1857.	1858.	1859.	1860.	1861.	1862.	1863.
Austria-Hungary					13	78	93
Belgium	1,011	160	137	30	100	124	136
Denmark	762	490	470	527	154	1,565	1,473
France	4,441	2,747	2,772	3,080	3,389	2,898	2,314
German Empire	86,407	69,586	46,635	43,946	52,116	23,811	29,741
Italy	1,046	1,414	1,051	920	954	621	514
Netherlands	986	1,201	168	342	369	339	349
Norway	1						20
Portugal	116	203	85	88	92	22	104
Russian Empire and Finland	74	108	314	156	129	134	135
Spain	637	922	1,454	974	804	381	336
Sweden	881	2,645	1,850	629	287	1,021	1,179
Switzerland	1,713	1,671	866	676	1,243	587	696
United Kingdom:							
England	27,060	21,013	15,188	12,838	13,207	7,659	13,615
Ireland	59,370	41,500	34,410	40,547	43,351	16,800	36,545
Scotland	3,833	3,202	1,981	1,995	1,244	730	954
Wales	601	492	320	547	564	366	632
Europe, not specified	20,191	16,823	11,884	12,633	13,771	7,055	33,432
Total Europe	209,130	164,177	119,585	119,928	131,777	64,191	122,268
China	4,524	7,183	3,215	6,117	6,094	4,174	5,280
Other Asia	4	5	1	8	14	7	9
Total Asia	4,528	7,188	3,216	6,125	6,108	4,181	5,289
Africa	26	8	20	119	48	8	12
British North America	6,068	5,360	4,544	4,412	3,221	2,538	3,388
Central America	277	11	5	7	9	31	8
Mexico	401	342	301	243	207	197	101
South America	85	130	116	204	148	90	139
West Indies	808	922	718	1,158	853	543	575
All other countries	9,223	13,804	1,066	947	506	404	1,145
Grand total	230,546	191,942	129,571	133,143	142,877	72,183	132,925

Country.	1864.	1865.	1866.	1867.	1868.	1869.	1870.
Austria-Hungary	136	518	87	392	553	1,499	4,425
Belgium	411	282	1,515	1,173	97	1,922	1,002
Denmark	738	772	1,092	2,031	1,596	3,649	4,083
France	2,128	2,949	5,724	5,886	6,119	3,879	4,007
German Empire	41,155	58,153	120,218	124,076	122,677	131,042	118,225
Italy	694	594	1,318	1,585	1,549	1,489	2,893
Netherlands	520	572	1,613	2,598	718	1,134	1,066
Norway	265	84	9,220	2,510	4,296	16,068	13,216
Portugal	48	383	249	320	294	87	255
Russian Empire and Finland	385	217	999	618	376	527	1,130
Spain	681	902	613	862	876	1,123	663
Sweden	1,192	2,500	2,840	5,919	11,253	24,224	13,443
Switzerland	1,022	1,738	3,751	4,656	3,405	3,650	3,075
United Kingdom:							
England	29,349	25,964	133,061	126,289	115,292	35,673	60,957
Ireland	69,161	51,018				40,786	56,996
Scotland	3,186	3,195				7,751	12,521
Wales	856	332				660	1,011
Europe, not specified	29,222	19,599	13	15	9	40,380	29,216
Total Europe	181,099	169,772	282,313	278,930	268,210	315,543	328,184
China	5,240	3,702	1,872	3,519	6,707	12,874	15,740
Other Asia	2	11	25	60	63	68	85
Total Asia	5,242	3,713	1,897	3,579	6,770	12,942	15,825
Africa	25	46	32	26	21	72	31
British North America	3,642	3,763	37,419	18,128	5,373	21,117	40,411
Central America	1	1	6	5	2	3	33
Mexico	78	139	244	237	292	320	463
South America	142	128	225	266	197	90	69
West Indies	494	743	988	891	839	2,237	1,679
All other countries	391	2,034	9,453	1,042	485	444	508
Grand total	191,114	180,389	332,577	303,104	282,189	352,768	387,203

TABLE X.—NUMBER AND NATIONALITIES OF IMMIGRANTS ARRIVED IN THE UNITED STATES FROM 1857 TO 1905, INCLUSIVE—Continued.

Country.	1871.	1872.	1873.	1874.	1875.	1876.	1877.
Austria-Hungary	4,887	4,410	7,112	8,850	7,658	6,276	5,396
Belgium	774	738	1,176	817	615	515	488
Denmark	2,015	3,690	4,931	3,082	2,656	1,547	1,695
France	3,137	9,317	14,798	9,643	8,321	8,002	5,856
German Empire	82,554	141,109	149,671	87,291	47,769	31,937	29,298
Italy	2,816	4,190	8,757	7,667	3,681	3,017	3,195
Netherlands	993	1,909	3,811	2,444	1,237	855	591
Norway	9,418	11,421	16,247	10,384	6,093	5,173	4,588
Portugal	290	416	24	60	763	471	1,291
Russian Empire and Finland	1,208	2,665	4,972	5,868	8,981	5,700	7,132
Spain	558	595	541	485	601	518	665
Sweden	10,699	13,464	14,303	5,712	5,573	5,603	4,991
Switzerland	2,269	3,650	3,107	3,093	1,814	1,549	1,686
United Kingdom:							
England	56,530	69,764	74,801	50,905	40,130	24,373	19,161
Ireland	57,439	68,732	77,344	53,707	37,957	19,675	14,569
Scotland	11,984	13,916	13,841	10,429	7,310	4,582	4,135
Wales	899	1,214	840	665	449	324	281
Europe, not specified	16,078	65	104	130	77	86	74
Total Europe	264,548	351,265	396,380	261,232	181,635	120,108	105,092
China	7,135	7,788	20,291	13,776	16,437	22,781	10,594
Other Asia	102	37	39	61	57	153	39
Total Asia	7,237	7,825	20,330	13,837	16,494	22,934	10,633
Africa	23	38	22	14	35	41	16
British North America	47,082	40,176	37,871	32,960	24,051	22,471	22,116
Central America	4	8	38	20	15	15	7
Mexico	402	569	606	386	610	631	445
South America	96	101	163	144	132	156	87
West Indies	1,251	1,351	1,657	1,829	1,832	1,413	1,390
All other countries	707	3,473	2,736	2,917	2,694	2,222	2,071
Grand total	321,350	404,806	459,803	313,339	227,498	169,986	141,857

Country.	1878.	1879.	1880.	1881.	1882.	1883.	1884.
Austria-Hungary	5,150	5,963	17,267	27,935	29,150	27,625	36,571
Belgium	354	512	1,232	1,766	1,431	1,450	1,676
Denmark	2,105	3,474	6,576	9,117	11,618	10,319	9,202
France	4,159	4,655	4,313	5,227	6,003	4,821	3,608
German Empire	29,313	34,602	84,638	210,485	250,630	194,786	179,676
Italy	4,344	5,791	12,354	15,401	32,160	31,792	16,510
Netherlands	608	753	3,340	8,597	9,517	5,249	4,198
Norway	4,759	7,345	19,895	22,705	29,101	23,398	16,974
Portugal	660	392	260	171	42	176	701
Russian Empire and Finland	3,595	4,942	7,191	10,655	21,590	11,920	17,226
Spain	457	457	389	484	378	262	299
Sweden	5,390	11,001	39,186	49,760	64,607	38,277	26,552
Switzerland	1,808	3,161	6,156	11,293	10,844	12,751	9,386
United Kingdom:							
England	18,405	24,183	59,454	65,177	82,394	63,140	55,918
Ireland	15,932	20,013	71,603	72,342	76,432	81,486	63,344
Scotland	3,502	5,225	12,640	15,168	18,937	11,859	9,060
Wales	243	543	1,173	1,027	1,656	1,597	901
Europe not specified	48	58	80	131	274	246	504
Total Europe	100,832	133,070	347,747	527,441	646,764	521,154	452,206
China	8,992	9,604	5,802	11,890	39,579	8,031	279
Other Asia	22	56	37	92	50	82	231
Total Asia	9,014	9,660	5,839	11,982	39,629	8,113	510
Africa	12	17	21	25	32	56	13
British North America	25,568	31,268	99,706	125,391	98,295	70,241	60,584
Central America	50	9	44	29	20	9	28
Mexico	465	556	492	325	366	469	430
South America	88	69	88	110	91	77	65
West Indies	1,019	1,123	1,351	1,680	1,291	908	2,208
All other countries	1,421	2,054	1,969	2,448	2,504	2,300	2,553
Grand total	138,469	177,826	457,257	669,431	788,992	603,322	518,592

TABLE X.—NUMBER AND NATIONALITIES OF IMMIGRANTS ARRIVED IN THE UNITED STATES FROM 1857 TO 1905, INCLUSIVE—Continued.

Country.	1885.	1886.	1887.	1888.	1889.	1890.	1891.
Austria-Hungary	27,309	28,680	40,265	45,814	34,174	56,199	71,042
Belgium	1,653	1,300	2,553	3,212	2,562	2,671	3,087
Denmark	6,100	6,225	8,524	8,962	8,699	9,366	10,659
France, including Corsica	3,495	3,318	5,034	6,454	5,918	6,585	6,770
German Empire	124,443	84,403	106,865	109,717	99,538	92,427	113,554
Gibraltar		8	12	18	13	9	13
Greece	172	104	313	782	158	524	1,105
Italy, including Sicily and Sardinia	13,642	21,315	47,622	51,558	25,307	52,003	76,055
Malta	4	7	1	3		1	6
Netherlands	2,689	2,314	4,506	5,845	6,460	4,326	5,206
Norway	12,356	12,759	16,269	18,264	13,390	11,370	12,568
Poland	3,085	3,939	6,128	5,826	4,922	11,073	27,497
Portugal, including CapeVerde and Azore islands	2,024	1,194	1,360	1,625	2,024	2,600	2,999
Roumania	803	494	2,045	1,186	893	517	957
Russian Empire and Finland	17,158	17,800	30,766	33,487	33,916	35,598	47,426
Spain	350	344	436	526	526	813	905
Sweden	22,248	27,751	42,836	54,698	35,415	29,632	36,880
Switzerland	5,895	4,805	5,214	7,737	7,070	6,993	6,811
Turkey in Europe	138	176	206	207	252	206	265
United Kingdom:							
England	47,332	49,767	72,855	82,574	68,503	57,020	53,600
Ireland	51,795	49,619	68,370	73,513	65,557	53,024	55,706
Scotland	9,226	12,126	18,699	24,457	18,296	12,041	12,557
Wales	1,127	1,027	1,820	1,654	1,181	650	424
Europe, not specified	39	54	130	12	16	32	43
Total Europe	353,083	329,529	482,829	538,131	484,790	445,680	546,085
China	22	40	10	26	118	1,716	2,836
Other Asia	176	277	605	817	1,607	2,732	4,842
Total Asia	198	317	615	843	1,725	4,448	7,678
Africa	112	122	40	65	187	112	103
Australia, Tasmania, New Zealand, and Pacific islands, not specified	679	1,136	1,282	2,387	2,196	1,167	1,301
British North America	38,291						
Central America	24	32	23	67	88	147	285
Mexico	323						
South America	44	246	366	440	427	438	664
West Indies	2,477	2,734	4,876	4,880	4,923	3,070	3,906
All other countries	115	87	78	76	91	240	297
Total immigrants	395,346	384,203	490,109	546,889	444,427	455,302	560,319

Country.	1892.	1893.	1894.	1895.	1896.	1897.	1898.
Austria-Hungary	76,937	57,420	38,638	33,401	65,103	33,031	39,797
Belgium	4,026	3,324	1,709	1,058	1,261	760	695
Denmark	10,125	7,720	5,003	3,910	3,167	2,085	1,946
France, including Corsica	4,678	3,621	3,080	2,628	2,463	2,107	1,990
German Empire	119,168	78,756	53,989	32,173	31,885	22,533	17,111
Greece	660	1,072	1,356	597	2,175	571	2,339
Italy, including Sicily and Sardinia	61,631	72,145	42,977	35,427	68,060	59,431	58,613
Netherlands	6,141	6,199	1,820	1,388	1,583	890	767
Norway	14,925	15,515	9,111	7,580	8,855	5,842	4,938
Poland	40,536	16,374	1,941	791	691	4,165	4,726
Portugal, including CapeVerde and Azores islands	3,400	4,631	2,196	1,452	2,766	1,874	1,717
Roumania			729	523	785	791	900
Russian Empire and Finland	81,511	42,310	39,278	35,907	51,445	25,816	29,828
Spain	4,078	206	925	501	351	448	577
Sweden	41,845	35,710	18,286	15,361	21,177	13,162	12,398
Switzerland	6,886	4,744	2,905	2,239	2,304	1,566	1,246
Turkey in Europe	1,331	625	298	245	169	152	176
United Kingdom:							
England	34,309	27,931	17,747	23,443	19,492	9,974	9,877
Ireland	51,383	43,578	30,231	46,304	40,262	28,421	25,128
Scotland	7,177	6,215	3,772	3,788	3,483	1,883	1,797
Wales	729	1,043	1,001	1,602	1,581	870	1,219
Europe, not specified			60	24	9	25	1
Total Europe	570,876	429,139	277,052	250,342	329,067	216,397	217,786

Table X.—Number and Nationalities of Immigrants Arrived in the United States from 1857 to 1905, inclusive—Continued.

Country.	1892.	1893.	1894.	1895.	1896.	1897.	1898.
China	(a)	472	1,170	539	1,441	3,363	2,071
Japan		1,380	1,931	1,150	1,110	1,526	2,230
Other Asia	(a)	540	1,589	2,806	4,213	4,773	4,336
Total Asia	(a)	2,392	4,690	4,495	6,764	9,662	8,637
Africa	(a)	(a)	24	36	21	37	48
Australia,Tasmania,New Zealand, and Pacific islands, not specified	(a)	(a)	244	141	112	199	201
British North America			194	239	273	290	350
Central America	(a)	(a)	32	21	17	6	7
Mexico			109	116	150	91	107
South America	(a)	(a)	39	36	35	49	39
West Indies	(a)	2,593	3,177	3,096	6,828	4,101	2,124
All other countries	8,787	5,606	70	14			
Total immigrants	579,663	439,730	285,631	258,536	343,267	230,832	229,299

Country.	1899.	1900.	1901.	1902.	1903.	1904.	1905.
Austria-Hungary	62,491	114,847	113,390	171,989	206,011	177,156	275,693
Belgium	1,101	1,196	1,579	2,577	3,450	3,976	5,302
Denmark	2,690	2,926	3,655	5,660	7,158	8,525	8,970
France, including Corsica	1,694	1,739	3,150	3,117	5,578	9,406	10,168
German Empire	17,476	18,507	21,651	28,304	40,086	46,380	40,574
Greece	2,333	3,771	5,910	8,104	14,090	11,343	10,515
Italy, including Sicily and Sardinia	77,419	100,135	135,996	178,375	230,622	193,296	221,479
Netherlands	1,029	1,735	2,349	2,284	3,998	4,916	4,954
Norway	6,705	9,575	12,248	17,484	24,461	23,808	25,064
Poland	(b)	(b)	(b)	(b)	(b)	(b)	(b)
Portugal, including Cape Verde and Azore islands	2,054	4,234	4,165	5,307	9,317	6,715	5,028
Roumania	1,606	6,459	7,155	7,196	9,310	7,087	4,437
Russian Empire and Finland	60,982	90,787	85,257	107,347	136,093	145,141	184,897
Servia, Bulgaria, and Montenegro	52	108	657	351	1,761	1,325	2,043
Spain	385	356	592	975	2,080	3,996	2,600
Sweden	12,797	18,650	23,331	30,894	46,028	27,763	26,591
Switzerland	1,326	1,152	2,201	2,344	3,983	5,023	4,269
Turkey in Europe	80	285	387	187	1,529	4,344	4,542
United Kingdom:							
England	10,402	9,951	12,214	13,575	26,219	38,626	64,709
Ireland	31,673	35,780	30,561	29,138	35,310	36,142	52,945
Scotland	1,724	1,792	2,070	2,560	6,143	11,092	16,977
Wales	1,324	764	701	763	1,275	1,730	2,503
Europe, not specified	6	2	18	37	5	143	13
Total Europe	297,349	424,700	469,237	619,068	814,507	767,933	974,273
China	1,660	1,247	2,459	1,649	2,209	4,309	2,166
Japan	2,844	12,635	5,269	14,270	19,968	14,264	10,331
Other Asia	4,468	4,064	5,865	6,352	7,789	7,613	11,428
Total Asia	8,972	17,946	13,593	22,271	29,966	26,186	23,925
Africa	51	30	173	37	176	686	757
Australia, Tasmania, New Zealand, and Pacific Islands, not specified			498	566	1,349	1,555	2,166
British North America	1,322	396	540	636	1,058	2,537	2,168
Central America	159	42	150	305	678	714	1,195
Mexico	161	237	347	709	528	1,009	2,637
South America	89	124	203	337	589	1,667	2,576
West Indies	2,585	4,656	3,176	4,711	8,170	10,193	16,641
All other countries	1,027	441	1	103	25	90	161
Total immigrants	311,715	448,572	487,918	648,743	857,046	812,870	1,026,499

a Included in all other countries.
b Beginning with 1899, Polish immigrants have been included in the countries to which they belong.

TABLE XI.—ALIENS (EXCLUSIVE OF ALIENS IN TRANSIT) ADMITTED, BY NATIONALI-
TIES, INTO THE UNITED STATES DURING THE CALENDAR YEAR ENDED DECEMBER
31, 1904.

Country.	Aliens.	Country.	Aliens.
Austria-Hungary	165,815	China	3,019
Belgium	4,292	Japan	12,225
Denmark	9,193	India	304
France, including Corsica	9,999	Turkey in Asia	5,731
German Empire	42,848	Other Asia	3,665
Greece	9,617		
Italy, including Sicily and Sardinia	156,794	Total Asia	24,844
Netherlands	4,766		
Norway	24,165	Africa	998
Portugal, including Cape Verde and		Australia, Tasmania, and New Zealand.	1,751
Azore islands	5,538	Philippine Islands	78
Roumania	5,154	Pacific islands, not specified	49
Russian Empire and Finland	161,649	British North America	2,584
Servia, Bulgaria, and Montenegro	1,252	British Honduras	132
Spain, including Canary and Balearic		Other Central America	867
islands	3,182	Mexico	1,924
Sweden	23,806	South America	2,100
Switzerland	4,461	West Indies	13,594
Turkey in Europe	3,101	All other countries	130
United Kingdom:			
England	57,382	Grand total	808,257
Ireland	49,420		
Scotland	14,467		
Wales	2,294		
Europe, not specified	11		
Total Europe	759,206		

Table XII gives the immigration of aliens for each year, beginning
with 1820 up to and including that for the fiscal year 1904, and the
two succeeding tables repeat the figures presented in Table VI, but
arranged with reference to the calendar year.

TABLE XII.—NUMBER OF IMMIGRANTS ARRIVED IN THE UNITED STATES EACH YEAR
FROM 1820 TO 1905, BOTH INCLUSIVE.

Period.	Number.	Period.	Number.
Year ending September 30—		Year ending December 31—	
1820	8,385	1851	379,466
1821	9,127	1852	371,603
1822	6,911	1853	368,645
1823	6,354	1854	427,833
1824	7,912	1855	200,877
1825	10,199	1856	195,857
1826	10,837	January 1 to June 30, 1857	112,123
1827	18,875	Year ending June 30—	
1828	27,382	1858	191,942
1829	22,520	1859	129,571
1830	23,322	1860	133,143
1831	22,633	1861	142,877
October 1, 1831, to December 31, 1832	60,482	1862	72,183
Year ending December 31—		1863	132,925
1833	58,640	1864	191,114
1834	65,365	1865	180,339
1835	45,374	1866	332,577
1836	76,242	1867	303,104
1837	79,340	1868	282,189
1838	38,914	1869	352,768
1839	68,069	1870	387,203
1840	84,066	1871	321,350
1841	80,289	1872	404,806
1842	104,565	1873	459,803
January 1 to September 30, 1843	52,496	1874	313,339
Year ending September 30—		1875	227,498
1844	78,615	1876	169,986
1845	114,371	1877	141,857
1846	154,416	1878	138,469
1847	234,968	1879	177,826
1848	226,527	1880	457,257
1849	297,024	1881	669,431
1850	310,004	1882	788,992
October 1 to December 31, 1850	59,976	1883	603,322

TABLE XII.—NUMBER OF IMMIGRANTS ARRIVED IN THE UNITED STATES EACH YEAR FROM 1820 TO 1905, BOTH INCLUSIVE—Continued.

Period.	Number.	Period.	Number.
Year ending June 30—Continued.		Year ending June 30—Continued.	
1884	518,592	1895	258,536
1885	395,346	1896	343,267
1886	334,203	1897	230,832
1887	490,109	1898	229,299
1888	546,889	1899	311,715
1889	444,427	1900	448,572
1890	455,302	1901	487,918
1891	560,319	1902	648,743
1892	579,663	1903	857,046
1893	439,730	1904	812,870
1894	285,631	1905	1,026,499

TABLE XIII.—REPORT OF ALIENS ADMITTED INTO THE UNITED STATES DURING THE SIX MONTHS ENDING DECEMBER 31, 1904.

Country.	Sex and number of aliens admitted.			Aliens in transit.	Grand total.
	Males.	Females.	Total.		
Austria-Hungary	55,375	34,002	89,377	973	90,350
Austria	21,594	14,909	36,503	407	36,910
Hungary	33,781	19,093	52,874	566	53,440
Belgium	1,567	918	2,485	89	2,574
Denmark	2,205	1,812	4,017	46	4,063
France, including Corsica	3,680	2,681	6,361	868	7,229
German Empire	12,020	10,024	22,044	528	22,572
Greece	2,408	236	2,644	31	2,675
Italy, including Sicily and Sardinia	28,267	14,982	43,249	490	43,739
Netherlands	1,112	626	1,738	32	1,770
Norway	5,192	4,987	10,179	96	10,275
Portugal, including Cape Verde and Azore islands.	959	729	1,688	20	1,708
Roumania	1,275	1,237	2,512	66	2,578
Russian Empire and Finland	58,315	27,876	86,191	1,065	87,256
Russian Empire	55,233	25,336	80,569	973	81,542
Finland	3,082	2,540	5,622	92	5,714
Servia, Bulgaria, and Montenegro	723	32	755	9	764
Spain, including Canary and Balearic islands	1,015	250	1,265	130	1,395
Sweden	5,648	7,645	13,293	118	13,411
Switzerland	1,206	864	2,070	32	2,102
Turkey in Europe	895	97	992	43	1,035
United Kingdom	44,168	37,924	82,092	3,401	85,493
England	25,808	15,343	41,151	2,716	43,867
Ireland	11,778	18,331	30,109	240	30,349
Scotland	5,659	3,580	9,239	405	9,644
Wales	923	670	1,593	40	1,633
Europe, not specified	3	3	6		6
Total Europe	226,033	146,925	372,958	8,037	380,995
China	1,405	92	1,497	584	2,081
Japan	4,500	654	5,154	575	5,729
India	57	17	74	17	91
Turkey in Asia	2,231	1,168	3,399	152	3,551
Other Asia	1,802	198	2,000	8	2,008
Total Asia	9,995	2,129	12,124	1,336	13,460
Africa	328	100	428	46	474
Australia, Tasmania, and New Zealand	619	240	859	262	1,121
Philippine Islands	33	3	36	1	37
Pacific Islands, not specified	16	3	19	17	36
British North America	1,452	254	1,706	1,023	2,729
British Honduras	43	27	70	20	90
Other Central America	347	122	469	203	672
Mexico	1,010	221	1,231	474	1,705
South America	912	351	1,263	416	1,679
West Indies	5,460	2,642	8,102	1,109	9,211
All other countries	60	28	88	15	103
Grand total	246,308	153,045	399,853	12,959	412,312

TABLE XIV.—REPORT OF ALIENS ADMITTED INTO THE UNITED STATES DURING THE SIX MONTHS ENDING JUNE 30, 1905.

Country.	Sex and number of aliens admitted.			Aliens in transit.	Grand total.
	Males.	Females.	Total.		
Austria-Hungary	142,182	44,134	186,316	1,824	188,140
Austria	54,594	20,893	75,487	1,102	76,589
Hungary	87,588	23,241	110,829	722	111,551
Belgium	1,987	830	2,817	125	2,942
Denmark	3,484	1,469	4,953	28	4,981
France, including Corsica	2,327	1,480	3,807	652	4,459
German Empire	11,328	7,202	18,530	473	19,003
Greece	7,608	263	7,871	102	7,973
Italy, including Sicily and Sardinia	154,451	23,779	178,230	3,343	181,573
Netherlands	2,107	1,109	3,216	97	3,313
Norway	10,660	4,225	14,885	172	15,057
Portugal, including Cape Verde and Azore Islands.	2,192	1,148	3,340	1	3,341
Roumania	989	986	1,925	50	1,975
Russian Empire and Finland	69,556	29,150	98,706	1,417	100,123
Russian Empire	60,812	26,547	87,359	1,316	88,675
Finland	8,744	2,603	11,347	101	11,448
Servia, Bulgaria, and Montenegro	1,267	21	1,288	15	1,303
Spain, including Canary and Balearic Islands	1,141	194	1,335	333	1,668
Sweden	8,763	4,535	13,298	119	13,417
Switzerland	1,488	711	2,199	58	2,257
Turkey in Europe	3,505	45	3,550	241	3,791
United Kingdom	33,546	21,496	55,042	5,258	60,300
England	15,468	8,090	23,558	4,195	27,753
Ireland	12,063	10,773	22,836	305	23,141
Scotland	5,388	2,350	7,738	709	8,447
Wales	627	283	910	49	959
Europe, not specified	6	1	7		7
Total Europe	458,587	142,728	601,315	14,308	615,623
China	616	53	669	770	1,439
Japan	4,605	572	5,177	219	5,396
India	98	18	116	20	136
Turkey in Asia	2,004	754	2,758	172	2,930
Other Asia	2,830	251	3,081	8	3,089
Total Asia	10,153	1,648	11,801	1,189	12,990
Africa	273	56	329	47	376
Australia, Tasmania, and New Zealand	806	426	1,232	300	1,532
Philippine Islands	3		3		3
Pacific Islands, not specified	12	5	17	30	47
British North America	365	97	462	1,242	1,704
British Honduras	34	19	53	23	76
Other Central America	404	199	603	336	939
Mexico	1,168	238	1,406	789	2,195
South America	954	359	1,313	420	1,733
West Indies	5,804	2,735	8,539	1,582	10,121
All other countries	43	30	73	31	104
Grand total	478,606	148,540	627,146	20,297	647,443

CONTRACT-LABOR LAW.

Of the various features of the immigration law none has proved so difficult of enforcement as that which was passed for the protection of labor in this country from unfair competition by aliens. This fact is due to causes that have been adverted to in former reports of the Bureau, but close observation convinces me that the chief obstacle is the erroneous impression that it is a measure wrung from Congress against its will by the power of organized labor, exacting all it could obtain rather than seeking simple justice. This impression, which is widely prevalent and produces, if not a hostile bias against the law, at least an indifference to its enforcement, does not credit the lawmaking branch of the Government with any worthier motive for enacting the contract-labor law than selfish fear. The public may, perhaps, discern and approve the economic wisdom of a protective tariff for the benefit of domestic manufactures and materials and credit Congress with a desire, in passing such laws, to benefit the entire country by vitalizing a sound principle of public policy, though the direct result is confessedly a benefit to certain classes and a corresponding charge in the first instance on the people at large. It fails to see, however, that Congress may have been equally influenced by principle, although labor is primarily the beneficiary, when it forbade those classes, which are the primary beneficiaries of a protective duty, to import alien labor and thus absorb all of the benefits of that duty, depriving labor of its due proportion of such benefit, and, in its larger aspect as relates to the peace and good order of the people as a whole, condemning to idleness, or to comparatively inadequate compensation, that large body of American citizens whose brawn, intelligence, and industry are such potent, such essential features of our national prosperity.

Because of such false impression the Bureau finds its efforts to enforce the law either reluctantly submitted to or resisted, actively or passively, and itself viewed as in some sort a branch or agency of organized labor, sensitive to that body's interest, responsive to its wishes, and thus essentially different from other parts of the executive government of the United States.

Perhaps labor is itself not altogether free from blame for this false public impression, and thus unconsciously has played into the hands of those interests which find it to their account to alienate public sympathy by encouraging such a view. At least on one occasion during the past year a branch of organized miners urged the Bureau that an offending company, upon which it had originally been active in fixing the responsibility for a violation of the law, should not be prosecuted because the said miners and the company had reached a settlement of their differences.

Despite these obstacles the Bureau has never relaxed its efforts to make the law effective. It can not, therefore, concede that the responsibility or fault rests with it when it reports its conviction that what should be the most effective feature of the contract-labor law is a complete failure. It is useless, as well as uncandid, to disguise the fact that it is virtually impossible to secure the conviction of those who induce the migration of alien laborers to this country under promise of employment here. The offenders are generally wealthy corporations, and have, as a rule, so shifted the responsibility for the offense from their own shoulders upon some minor employee without property, through the diversion of which he could be reached under the statutory penalty, that it is almost impossible to establish the relation of principal and agent between the offenders, respectively, in intent and in act.

But there are other cases where the proof of the offense seems convincing and beyond doubt. These cases, however, for reasons not relating to the functions of the Bureau, can not be brought to trial until the witnesses are dispersed beyond reach, and so the Government is compelled to choose between the two equally futile courses of dismissing the proceedings or submitting to defeat. As an instance of such cases the Bureau will refer to the case against the San Francisco Brick Company, mentioned in its last annual report. The case was then more than a year old. After the expiration of another twelve-month, it seems to be no nearer to a conclusion, the demurrers to the bills of complaint having been filed in March, 1904, and remaining undecided as yet by the court.

Another case, also referred to in the last report of the Bureau, that against the Ellsworth Mining Company, of Pennsylvania, was continued by counsel for the Government until the witnesses have been dispersed beyond reach. As a result there remains nothing to be done except to dismiss the suits, thus again illustrating the futility of the Bureau's efforts to secure the punishment of violators of this law, who are almost invariably wealthy and influential corporations.

It will be obvious from what has been said that the Bureau is able to accomplish something only under that provision of the act which is remedial. Such aliens as the officers can show to have been induced to come to this country under promise of employment are excluded, if possible. Their number is necessarily small, because the evidence to establish the unlawful inducement to their migration must be obtained usually from their own confessions; and aliens of sufficient capacity to justify the expense and risk of importation are as a rule of exceptional intelligence, and have been invariably warned of the necessity of devising plausible stories which prevent the inspectors from ascertaining the truth.

Even in those cases in which the vigilance of inspectors avails to discredit the false testimony and secure a confession of the truth from such aliens, the contracting company comes forward, enters an appeal to the Department from the excluding decision of the board of special inquiry, employs able counsel, and uses other available means to impress upon the Government a proper sense of its financial and political influence. On appeal learned counsel deny any contract or promise with his client's knowledge or authority; declares that the appellants perjured themselves, but suggests that perjury is not a ground under the law for exclusion; disclaims any knowledge of the reasons for such perjury; declares that the company he represents needs the men excluded by the board and can not obtain such labor in this country. Upon the issue as to whether labor is accessible in this country for the uses to which the imported aliens are to be put, it is not difficult to perceive that one may easily be misled. It will be recalled that in one such case, involving the capacity of American three-color etchers or engravers, the importing company excused itself for refusing to go into the details of the process it used to enable the Department to make a comparison with systems now in operation in this country, upon the score that its process was a trade secret.

In view of what has been said, it will be surprising to learn that out of the one million and odd of arriving aliens so many have been detected by the inspectors and denied admission as provided by law.

This subject has been treated at some length because the Bureau feels that it is one of great importance, involving not alone the interests of labor, but as well the material interests of the country, and, above all else, the vital question of respect for and obedience to the constitutionally expressed will of the people of this country. It can not, either by silence or by vague and brief comments, allow the confessed inefficiency of the alien contract labor law to be charged in any degree to neglect or to perfunctory action by it. The obstructions it has endeavored and is endeavoring to surmount have therefore been fully set forth herein,

DISEASED ALIENS.

As elsewhere stated in this report, the provisions of section 9 of the immigration act of 1903 continue to prove ineffective in restraining the steamship companies from bringing to our ports aliens suffering with communicable diseases.   One device of the companies to escape the payment of the fine imposed and yet secure the passage money of such aliens was pointed out last year.   Whether that, or other devices of a similar nature, is still used the Bureau has no means of knowing, but it directs attention to the fact that the increase in diseased alien passengers over the number reported a year ago, 1,560, is about 41 per cent.

The accompanying table shows the proportion contributed by each race to the total of such immigration for the year to which this report relates, as well as for the next preceding fiscal year.

Race.	1904.	1905.	Race.	1904.	1905.
Hebrew	183	353	Chinese	41	74
Japanese	196	285	Slovak	38	66
Italian (south)	235	247	Armenian	30	50
Polish	173	204	Finnish	48	46
Syrian	115	155	Scandinavian	34	43
Magyar	29	103	Italian (north)	35	41
German	99	100	All others	190	251
Lithuanian	89	92			
Croatian and Slovenian	25	88	Total	1,560	2,198

The particular disease from which most of these aliens suffered is trachoma, a highly contagious disease of the eye, which is particularly of oriental origin.   In some instances Chinese persons, of professedly high caste, have been refused admission because they were afflicted with trachoma and not because of any defect in their right to admission under the Chinese-exclusion laws.

That the abuse referred to has not grown greater in consequence of any administrative laxity in punishing the offense will appear from the accompanying table, which shows that $27,300 have been collected during the year for violations of section 9 aforesaid.

FINES CERTIFIED UNDER SECTION 9, FISCAL YEAR 1905.

Port.	July.	August.	September.	October.	November.	December.
Baltimore					$200	$500
Boston	$200	$300	$700	$100		600
Key West						
New Orleans				200		
New York	1,400	2,400	800	1,200	1,700	2,100
Philadelphia	400	400	700	1,100		400
San Francisco		100	100			
Total	2,000	3,200	2,300	2,600	1,900	3,600

Port.	January.	February.	March.	April.	May.	June.	Total.
Baltimore	$300	$800	$600	$200	$400		$3,000
Boston	600		200			$200	2,900
Key West						200	200
New Orleans	100		200			100	600
New York	1,900	1,100	500	600	500	1,900	16,100
Philadelphia	100	200	100	300		100	3,800
Portland, Me.				300			300
San Francisco			200				400
Total	3,000	2,100	1,800	1,400	900	2,500	27,300

The last report of the Bureau set forth fully the evils resulting from this abuse. It is not necessary, therefore, to repeat them here. If the amendment to the law, recommended hereinafter, increasing the penalty, is adopted, or if the suggested limitation on the number of aliens that may be brought on any vessel becomes law, the Bureau is sanguine that, if accompanied by competent medical inspection at the ports of foreign embarkation, this abuse will virtually cease.

INDUCEMENTS TO IMMIGRATION.

The figures presented by the statistical reports for the year under consideration have now attained such dimensions as to challenge painstaking consideration of their import. It is impossible that such an influx can fail to produce material effects upon the institutions of this country, as it is doing upon the population. What such effects will probably be in the long run, it is not within the proper scope of this report to discuss; but attention is drawn to the subject to show that, if it is the public desire to establish some reasonable limitation on immigration, some restriction that will materially lessen the volume of the current until, by actual experience assurance is secured of the safety of the institutions of the country under such an unexampled strain, it is time to make a new departure in legislating upon alien immigration. It is no longer sufficient to close the door upon certain classes, manifestly undesirable additions to any community. The aliens who are forbidden admission to the United States by section 2 of the act of March 3, 1903, are as objectionable to the communities in which they were born and of which they have always formed a part as they are to us. It can not be denied, however, that of such as are not expressly excluded by law there are many aliens entering the United States who, if not individually open to objection on the score of physical, mental, or moral defects admitted of all men, are yet of such totally alien, if not repugnant, character and genius as to raise a doubt whether they will in the present or the succeeding generation become assimilated in customs and ideals to the people of this country. This view has found expression as yet in legislation affecting aliens of but one race. That solitary instance, however, is a recognition of the principle that the public welfare at this stage of the world's development demands the intervention of the law-making branch of the Government to prevent an unrestricted irruption of elements hostile to our institutions, if not incapable of comprehending them.

The difficulties and embarrassments that have been experienced in the administration of that unique legislation, however, suggest the expediency of first attempting by other means to check the enormous and miscellaneous immigration now pouring, practically without check as to numbers, into our seaports and across our land borders. The Government has control, through its authority over our ports, of the transportation agencies by which aliens are brought to this country, and, unless it be conceded that our commercial interest is paramount to all other considerations and clothes those great corporations which are its vehicles with a sanctity of right which it is impious to question or restrict, the natural and sensible recourse from the present dangers is to place some reasonable restriction upon them. What such restrictions should be must be left to the wisdom of Congress; but it is not the design of this report, in pointing out this course, to place the

Bureau on record as holding hostile views to the transportation lines or as advocating any further restraints upon their business than will suffice to protect the United States from an energy that knows no rest and a singleness of purpose which considers no results except those of a financial nature.

For several years past the Bureau has called attention in its annual reports to the vast organization of foreign agencies, those working as a part of the transportation lines and those working as volunteers on a commission basis, and has fortified its statements by the reports of its officers sent abroad from time to time for the purpose of securing information as to the causes leading to immigration. Such reports are abundantly avouched by exhibits showing the efforts, not alone of private individuals, but of some foreign governments as well, to secure passengers for the various competing lines of ocean steamers. When such efforts result in an addition to our alien population within one year of more than a million souls, when they occasion such an over-taxing of the carrying accommodations of steamships as to produce violations of our navigation laws, and when they give occasion for such disregard by these ocean carriers of sanitary laws as results in need-less deaths aboard ship, the dissemination of disease among the passengers, and the introduction of contagion into this country—then the time would appear to have come for the intervention of the Government, not to restrict the vested rights of capital, but to prevent the agencies by which those rights are exercised from violating rights equally sacred and of more enduring importance to the well-being of the people of this country.

In another part of this report this matter is considered in connection with the subject of diseased and physically defective immigrants, but it seems not inappropriate to quote here, from a report of one of the Bureau's officers, the following typical incident:

Recently one of the ladies connected with the Associated Charities of the District of Columbia called at the Bureau to ascertain whether the immigration authorities could take any action looking to the deportation of a certain Hungarian family located in Washington, and as the story narrated by this lady is an interesting one, it is thought best to report it as briefly as possible:

The entire family, consisting of husband, wife, and five children, had been located in Hungary, the husband being engaged as a barber and the wife as a hairdresser. They were in much better circumstances than the average Hungarian peasant, and were both prosperous and happy. A representative of one of the steamship companies called upon the father and represented to him that while he was doing nicely in his present situation he could do twice as well in America. Believing this story, he left his wife and children and came to Baltimore. Finding that the wages paid barbers in Baltimore were scarcely adequate to his own support, he came to Washington and obtained a position at $10 a week. This salary enabled him to send small amounts to his wife from time to time, and he wrote her in a rather encouraging way, although he did not himself feel that he had been particularly benefited by coming to the United States.

The wife, thinking that her husband was realizing the expectations created in their minds by the steamship agent, disposed of their business and household effects and came to Baltimore without having notified her husband, evidently thinking it would be a pleasant surprise to him. He was surprised to receive a telegram that they had arrived, but the surprise was anything but pleasant. He, of course, proceeded to Baltimore, and upon his testifying before the board that he was steadily employed at $10 a week the wife and five children were admitted to his care and proceeded with him to this city.

The wife, of course, immediately realized the serious error into which she had fallen and became almost crazed through distress and homesickness, and, in the opinion of the lady who narrated the story, it will only be a short period of time before she must be confined to some institution for the insane. Thus, a happy and prosperous family of Europe have been thrown into physical and mental distress and have been induced to sacrifice their business and household effects because of the desire of a steamship agent to increase his business by selling the several passages involved in moving the family to America.

The representative of the Associated Charities was, of course, advised that there was nothing that the immigration officials could do to assist her protégés, and she thereupon stated that she would endeavor to raise a sufficient fund among the Hungarian residents of Washington to pay the return passage of the entire family to their native country.

As a further corroboration of the views reiterated under this head, the following report of one of the Bureau's special inspectors is given:

NEW YORK, *September 5, 1905.*

SIR: In accordance with your authorization and instructions in Department letter No. 48195, dated February 28, 1905, I embarked April 19 on the steamship *Majestic* bound for Liverpool.   *   *   *

I at first covered the English ports, especially Liverpool and Southampton, witnessing the embarkation of emigrants on the steamers of the White Star Line, the American Line, and the Allan Line.   I also made a detailed study in Liverpool of the various boarding houses maintained by the steamship companies and their authorized agents and "runners."   I paid special attention to the treatment of emigrants afflicted with trachoma by physicians employed by the steamship companies, their agents and "runners," for the purpose of preparing diseased aliens for safe passage through the inspection of the marine-hospital surgeons at the ports of debarkation in the United States.

On the whole I can state that, with the exceptions to be noted hereafter, my observations have shown that every company tries its best to have all emigrants examined by a physician to determine their admissibility to the United States, knowing, as they do, that it is rather expensive to bring a deported immigrant back to England, and in addition to pay $100 fine for each case of trachoma.   The physicians representing the companies are expected to determine who, notwithstanding the fact that his scalp and eyes are not in perfect order, can still be passed through the vigilant inspection of the immigration authorities in the United States.   It is also the duty of the authorized physicians of the companies to treat and "cure" such cases of trachoma and favus as may within a reasonable time be "fixed" up and prepared so that the diseased alien may have a reasonable chance to enter the United States.   All this latter is done for such emigrants as have a sufficient amount of money to pay for several weeks' board and lodging and for the medical attendance.

The emigrants arrive in Liverpool almost daily in groups varying from a score to over 100.   On the day before the sailing of a steamer the largest number usually arrives.   They are met by the companies' agents and conducted to boarding houses maintained or subsidized by the steamship companies.   The proprietor or manager of each boarding house is also an authorized agent to sell steamship tickets to the emigrants, which is of great importance, as will appear hereafter.   In these boarding houses the companies' doctors call the day before the sailing of a steamship and examine every emigrant, with a view to determine his admissibility.   In Liverpool this medical examination is usually made by the physician who accompanies the steamship across the ocean—the ship's surgeon—and can by no means be designated as thorough—first, because the ship's surgeon is, as a rule, not qualified to determine the presence of trachoma in doubtful cases; and, second, because the boarding-house keeper is present and does his best to pass all those who bought tickets from him. Some of these boarding-house keepers are well known in Liverpool as being especially qualified to pass diseased aliens who would otherwise be rejected.   It must be mentioned, however, that the steamship companies often resent the imposition by these agents after being compelled to pay $100 fine for each case of trachoma thus passed.   In some cases agents were known to send aboard a ship emigrants who had repeatedly been rejected by the doctors, and even such as had been deported by the immigration authorities in the United States.   While in Liverpool I was shown that the agents have been fined by the steamship companies for just such acts, but they continue to act as official representatives of the companies.

All those who are isolated by the doctors as being inadmissible remain in the boarding house, ostensibly for the purpose of transportation in the near future to their native homes.   This is done with such emigrants as have no money or can not write home for additional funds.   But those who have a surplus of money above the usual price charged for a steamship ticket from Liverpool to New York, Boston, or Philadelphia, are kept in the boarding house and placed in charge of a physician, officially appointed by the steamship companies to treat cases of trachoma and prepare them for safe passage through the inspection by the marine-hospital surgeons in the United States. Dr. David Morgan, of 46 Nelson street, Liverpool, acting for the Cunard Line, treated many cases of trachoma in my presence at Heilborn's and Mrs. Maddock's Cunard hotels. Some of these emigrants had been under treatment for over one month. They usually pay 2 shillings and 6 pence per day for board and lodging; 1 shilling for each medical treatment. One boarding house is particularly notorious in this regard. It is kept by a native of Malta—Andrew Barber, 5 Kent street W. When I visited it I found there over 50 emigrants, mostly Armenians, Italians, and Greeks, each of whom had been refused transportation at continental ports. This man Barber told me that he could pass anybody. He has "doctors who can cure;" he sends them for examination in groups of 10 or 12, 8 of whom are healthy and 2 or 4 are sick. It is his experience that the steamship companies' doctors examine the first cases thoroughly, but the last few they generally pass quickly. He told me that he undertakes to land in the United States anybody who has been rejected at continental ports. He has passed many who have previously even been deported by the immigration authorities in the United States.

On embarkation the emigrants are again examined by the steamship doctor and also by a doctor of the board of trade. The former, acting for the steamship companies, is usually careless and will pass anybody. The contrary appears to be true of the board of trade physicians. In my presence, while emigrants were embarking on the *Cymric*, White Star Line, on Friday, April 28, Dr. J. De Vere Hill, acting for the board of trade, discovered two cases of deformities of the hands, a case of chickenpox, a case of locomotor ataxia, and one of paralysis. All these cases had been passed by the steamship doctor as healthy and admissible under the immigration laws of the United States. But it must be remembered that the board of trade doctor examines only for such contagious diseases as may be dangerous for the crew, and trachoma is not included under this term as understood by the board of trade in Liverpool. From the attached photographs it will be seen that for favus neither doctor is looking at all—most of the emigrants are passing with covered heads. Another feature of the examination which is of importance is the presence of the runners on board trying to help the doctors. * * *

It is the prevailing conviction of all of the runners in Liverpool and London that the authorities in New York City are too severe, and that it is dangerous to attempt to send diseased aliens to that port. Deportation is very certain. But they are convinced that the ports of Boston, and particularly Philadelphia, are very easy. In fact, every agent and runner I interviewed informed me that he could guarantee the admission of any alien afflicted with trachoma if sent on one of the steamers of the American Line to Philadelphia. For such a guaranty an agent asked an additional sovereign. How they can accomplish this in Philadelphia I am unable to state, but I have been assured that such is the case. In the White Chapel district in London I saw many porters in front of ticket agencies announcing that the particular agents would pass anybody into the United States. I transmitted one such handbill to you with a previous communication. In that handbill the agent promises to open "all the doors of the United States," and proclaims that under his guidance deportation is impossible.

In London and Liverpool the clinics of the eye infirmaries are daily crowded with aliens who are being treated for trachoma, expecting to go to the United States as soon as "cured." There is also a large number of quacks who prey upon the unfortunates by promising to cure them, and thus cheat them out of their last penny. It must be remembered that many of the emigrants who are rejected at continental ports and who do not want to return to their native lands go to England. Here they try to obtain passage for the United States. A large proportion of these I am told are sent via Canada, where they are met by agents of the runner and often safely conducted to the United States. Others pass the medical examination at Southampton and Liverpool and try to gain admission through Boston or Philadelphia. Others still, and these are the worst cases of trachoma, remain in London for a shorter or longer time, where they submit to treatment in various infirmaries, often by quacks.

I have particularly investigated the question as to what becomes of all those emigrants who are rejected by the steamship doctors or are deported by the immigration authorities in the United States. After a careful inquiry and repeated interviews with such unfortunates, and also representatives of various charitable institutions in London and Liverpool, I can report as follows:

A small proportion try to be cured in the manner stated above and thus prepare themselves for safe passage to the United States. Others settle in England and give up the idea of ever going to America. Others still go to Canada to settle either permanently or temporarily, with a view to ultimately reaching the United States in some manner.   Others, again, go to South America, particularly Brazil and Argentina.   The representatives of the Jewish board of guardians and the "Jews' Temporary Shelter," assured me that they had discontinued helping people to go to the United States.   They send their cases to Argentina if they send them at all.   Interviews with emigrants at the "Shelter" confirmed such to be a fact.   All I spoke to told me that they were going to either South America or Canada.

In Antwerp every emigrant is carefully examined by several doctors before he is allowed to embark.   There the steamship company has an excellent staff of specialists, who are assisted by a doctor representing the Government emigration service.   The examination leaves nothing to be desired.

The bulk of the eastern European emigrants, and a fair proportion of the north and south Europeans, pass through Germany while emigrating for the United States.   The German steamship companies have taken special sanitary measures in dealing with the emigrants.   With the assistance of the police department of the Empire the emigrants are rigidly inspected.   This is especially regulated along the frontier of Russia and Austria-Hungary.   There have been established so-called "control stations" along the Russian borders in the following frontier towns: Bajohren, Tilsit, Insterburg, Eydtkuhnen, Prostken, Illowo, Ottlotschin, Posen, and Ostrovo, and also one in Ruhleben, near Berlin.   Along the Austro-Hungarian border "registration stations" have been established in Myslowitz, Ratibor, and Leipzig.   The object of these "control" and "registration" stations is to regulate transmigrants from a sanitary and police standpoint.

To begin with, the German Government does not permit these transmigrants from eastern Europe to stop over in any city of the Empire.   When the cholera epidemic was raging in Hamburg in 1894 the Russian transmigrants were charged with having imported the disease into the city, and strong measures have ever since been taken to prevent Russian emigrants from entering Germany, except under strict police surveillance.   This, of course, threatened the German steamship companies with the loss of a very lucrative business.   The emigrants not admitted to Germany might be compelled to go on vessels of other countries.   They solved the problem by undertaking to perfectly isolate all transmigrants.   Thus the above enumerated "control stations" originated.   As soon as a Russian emigrant crosses the frontier he is practically placed under arrest by a gendarme and kept under arrest until he embarks on the steamship bound for the country of his destination.   The process is as follows:

At all the railroad stations on the border of Germany, Russia, and Austria a special squad of gendarmerie is detailed to arrest every one who travels third or fourth class, and who appears to be a foreigner, and bring him to the agents of the steamship companies at their offices in the control stations.   Here the emigrant is rigidly interrogated as to what he is doing in Germany.   If he claims he intends to remain in the Empire for a certain time he is asked to prove that he will not become a public charge; that he has some legitimate business to attend to, etc.   If he can not satisfy the police, and particularly the steamship agent, in this respect, he is deported to Russia or Austria by the first train.   The vast majority of the Russian and Austrian third and fourth class passengers, however, state that they are transmigrants destined to the United States, England, Canada, Argentina, etc.   As such they are handed over in charge of the representatives of the steamship companies.   The latter at once inquire whether the transmigrants are provided with sufficient funds to pay for transportation to the country to which bound.   If so, as is the case with the largest proportion, they are at once told to procure railroad and steamship tickets.   After all these preliminaries, the emigrants who paid for the transportation are referred to the building called a "control station."   Here they are first conducted to the "bath," of which there are two departments, one for men and one for women.   All their clothing is removed and placed in a sterilizer for disinfection.   Each man, woman, and child is given a bath and rubbed down with green soap by special attendants.·   The doctor acting for the steamship companies is always present while the emigrants are being bathed, and examines every one with a view to detect any bodily deformity which may be covered by the clothing.   The sterilized clothing is then returned to the emigrants, and after dressing they are conducted to the "clean side" of the station, where they are kept until the departure of the train to Hamburg or Bremen.

Any emigrant found by the doctor to be afflicted with trachoma or favus is denied transportation and ordered to return to his native land.   If he refuses, he is handed over to the gendarme, who takes him, forcibly if necessary, to the frontier.   That this, however, is not done with all cases of trachoma and favus will appear hereafter.   All the emigrants who have passed the medical examination are sent to Hamburg or Bremen by the first train.   Upon reaching these cities they are met by representatives of the steamship companies and at once conducted, in Bremen, to special boarding houses maintained or subsidized by the steamship companies, and in Hamburg to the "Auswanderer Hallen." This latter is one of the most remarkable institutions and deserves a detailed description. The "Auswanderer Hallen" also has its origin in the charge made by the citizens of Hamburg that the transmigrants introduced cholera into the city during 1893. The steamship companies met this charge by promising to isolate the emigrants from the city, and built the "Hallen" for that purpose. It is located outside of the city on a plat of ground 25,000 square meters in dimensions, and is so situated that the emigrants reach it by special rail tracks and are able to embark on tenders when they leave Germany without ever coming into the city of Hamburg. It is divided into two main parts—the "unclean" and the "clean." The "unclean division" is for new arrivals, who are here bathed and their clothing and baggage disinfected, after which they are admitted to the "clean division," which consists of neat sleeping barracks, restaurants, churches, etc., where the emigrants are kept practically prisoners until the departure of a steamer. On the day of their departure the emigrants are again examined medically, with a special view to the detection of the presence of trachoma or favus. All such as are found suffering with loathsome or dangerous contagious diseases or are of poor physique are refused transportation and returned to their native lands. The German Government does not permit these emigrants to remain in any city of the Empire, and as they are practically prisoners in charge of the steamship companies (somewhat like "bonded" merchandise) the company is charged with the responsibility of disposing of them in some manner. I can state, however, after a thorough study of the question, that very few, comparatively speaking, return to their native lands. The vast majority of those rejected embark for England or South America. In the former country they often remain permanently, but occasionally try to prepare themselves for safe passage and admission to the United States. They quite often succeed, as I have mentioned above, while speaking of conditions in London and Liverpool.

Very little is done in Hamburg and Bremen to prepare emigrants for safe passage to the United States. Only rarely will a doctor treat an emigrant for trachoma or favus. But in the "control stations" along the Russian and Austrian borders the practice is very common. I have personally met over 50 trachomatous emigrants in the "Diakonesea Heim," the hospital in Thorn. All were refused health certificates by the physician acting for the steamship companies and told to return to their native homes. But, stating that they had enough money for a "cure," Mr. J. S. Caro had them admitted to the hospital. There they are being treated by physicians and are under the constant care of Miss Caro, the daughter of the agent of the steamship companies. Some emigrants told me that they had remained there for over two months; very few are "cured" in less than one month. They pay 3 marks per day for the use of the hospital and 2 marks for medical treatment. The same is the condition in several of the other cities where the "control stations" of the steamship companies are located.

Another disagreeable feature regarding the steamship agents which ought to be discontinued is the following: They look upon every eastern European emigrant as one who must go to the United States whether he desires to or not. Many of the emigrants arriving in Germany who are brought by the police to the "control stations," on being asked where they are bound for, say that they are en route to England. The agent sees very little commission in the sale of the ticket for London, and besides this suspects that the emigrant intends upon his arrival in England to embark on a vessel owned by one of the English or American companies. The emigrant passing through Germany is considered the legitimate prey of the German steamship companies and their agents. Conversations, such as the following, have often been overheard in "control stations."

Agent: "Where are you bound for?"
Emigrant: "To America."
Agent: "How much money have you?"
Emigrant: "How is that your business?"
Gendarme: "Don't talk back; show all the money you have. If you don't, I will at once take you back to Russia and hand you over to the authorities."

The poor bulldozed emigrant takes out all the money he has from the various places where he keeps it concealed. The agent counts it in the presence of the policeman. Then he deducts the price of transportation, fourth class, to Hamburg or Bremen and a steerage ticket to New York. What remains he exchanges for German money and returns it to the emigrant, who is not permitted to ask any more questions. Such is the case with the largest number of emigrants; but some on being asked where they are bound for state: "To England;" "To Belgium;" "To France." The agent will never believe it. He looks at every one as an "American" (the technical term applied to emigrants bound for the United States), and at once tells him: "You are a liar," insisting that his victim is bound for an American port and should buy a steamship ticket at once. I have personally witnessed at Thorn the case of a man, his wife, and four grown-up children who stated to the agent, Mr. Caro, that they had sold everything in their native home in Warsaw, Poland, and got together sufficient money to go to England. But Caro insisted that they ought to go to America and refused to sell tickets to England. The gendarme, representing the police department, sided with the agent. "Either go to New York or return to Poland" was the verdict. The poor man at last decided to send his wife and two daughters back to Poland, and he and his two sons bought tickets for New York. This is no isolated case. Every alien in Germany who is brought to a "control station" and who states that he intends to go to England is coerced by the steamship agents, with the assistance of the police, to go to the United States, and this coercion swells the number of emigrants to this country. Many who honestly want to settle in England thus find themselves traveling to the United States. I urgently recommend that the Department investigate this feature of the problem and find some remedy to put a stop to such disgraceful practices. Many an alien is picked up in Leipzig, Thorn, Eydtkuhnen, Berlin, Hamburg, etc., taken to the "control station," and told that he must go either to his native land or to America. No amount of pleading on the part of the unfortunate alien is of avail. He is not sold a ticket to England, France, or any other country. "America or home" is the verdict of the steamship company's agent, and the gendarme concurs.

A few more words about the German method of dealing with the emigrant. As I have described above, every emigrant is given a bath and his belongings are disinfected. This is done only to the poorer class who travel third or fourth class on the railroads and steerage on the steamships. All such as can pay the price of the second-class ticket are permitted to pass freely and are not subjected to any annoyance by doctors or police. Many aliens who have reason to fear a medical examination take advantage of this laxity and travel second class, thus securing passage to the United States. Often the steamship agent advises such aliens as are affected with trachoma to try second class, assuring them that it is very safe. This practice is more common on the French line. Every emigrant traveling steerage by this line is examined medically with a view to discovering the presence of trachoma, and all such as are refused transportation are at once taken in charge by the "runners," ostensibly for the purpose of sending them back to their native lands. In reality the emigrant is at once informed that if he has more money he can secure passage. First he must "dress up" a little more decently, and then secure a second-class ticket. Several runners in Havre have assured me that this method is quite safe, and that only exceptionally are second-class emigrants deported. It appears that in Havre it is only a question of money. Once one has the price, there is nothing that will disqualify him.

In Marseilles the "treatment" of trachoma has assumed quite remarkable dimensions. Here most of the emigrants from the Orient, from Syria, Armenia, etc., come on their way to the United States. Most of the Orientals report to one Anton Fares, who refers them to a boarding house. After the usual preliminaries, such as inquiries as to the amount of money in their possession, their destination, etc., the emigrants are referred to Doctor Reynaut for examination. Those who are found free from contagious disease are given tickets and at once sent to Havre. As is well known, these races are especially prone to trachoma and in a large proportion of instances the doctor does discover its presence. These are given by M. Fares the choice of two alternatives: Either to go via St. Nazaire to Mexico, where Fares claims to have agents who conduct them across the frontier to the United States, which is quite an expensive and tedious process, and of late very uncertain, or submit to a course of treatment by Dr. G. Reynaut, 20 Boulevard d'Athénée, Marseilles, who claims to have been very successful. A visit any day at 11 a. m. to this doctor's clinic will convince anyone that he does a flourishing business. I met more than 100 emigrants every day I visited this clinic. The charge is 1 franc for each treatment. Some of these unfortunate patients told me that they had been under treatment for over two months. The average duration of the treatment, however, is about two weeks, after which they are generally sent to Havre and thence shipped to New York. Another feature of this so-called treatment, which is, as far as I have observed, peculiar to Marseilles and Fares, is that many healthy emigrants who have no trachoma at all are under treatment for this disease. These are usually individuals who have money. Fares refers such persons to the doctor, who tells them that they have trachoma, but are curable. One franc a day for treatment, 3 or 4 francs for board and lodging for about a month is extracted from such an unfortunate. When finally he is pronounced cured he is charged more than the usual price for a steamship ticket. Such individuals are, as a rule, never deported for eye disease, and, believing that they had trachoma and that the doctor and Fares had cured them and safely passed them through the gates of the United States, are afterwards excellent advertisements among their countrymen for Fares.

This runner, Fares, is well known to the authorities in France. He has repeatedly been under charges for cheating emigrants, and Mr. J. Lespre, "Commissaire spécial des chemins de fer des ports et de l'émigration," in Marseilles told me that he gives him a great deal of trouble and requires vigilant watching. Many of Fares' acts have been brought to the attention of the French minister of the interior, and on three occasions it has been decreed to expel him from French territory. * * * I asked Mr. Lespre, the commissioner of emigration, how he explained Fares' presence in French territory after the ministry of the interior had within nine years served three orders of expulsion. "Well, there are certain powers at work; the steamship companies need him here," was the answer. In fact, Fares' newspaper, Al-Mircad, has a wide circulation in Syria and is in character a good advertising sheet for emigration to America. * * * He ships about 40 to 50 immigrants weekly, and stops at nothing in his dealing with them; and the steamship companies approve of everything he does. Whenever he is brought in conflict with the emigration authorities the Compagnie Générale Transatlantique is sure to come to his rescue.

The examination of emigrants in the south of Italy is conducted by the Marine-Hospital Service of the United States. Dr. Allan McLaughlin, passed assistant surgeon, Dr. Albert D. Foster, and an Italian physician, Dr. E. Buonocore, examine every emigrant who embarks in Naples. In Genoa and in Palermo they also have Italian physicians representing them. I need not report any details about their work, because everyone who has witnessed the work of the Marine-Hospital Service at Ellis Island, in Philadelphia, and in Boston knows how efficaciously it is conducted. Both Doctor McLaughlin and Doctor Foster have previously worked at Ellis Island and in Naples, and are doing their work exactly as similar work is being done in the United States. Their vigilance is evidenced by the following figures, showing the number of emigrants examined by them during 1900-1905:

Year.	Emigrants examined.	Rejected.
1900-1901	96,368	1,949
1901-2	169,218	5,639
1902-3	173,682	10,065
1903-4	165,537	5,225
1904-5	189,117	4,956
Total	793,922	27,834

It appears from these figures that during the five years ending June, 1905, 793,922 have been examined by the surgeons of the United States Marine-Hospital Service and 27,834 have been rejected, amounting to 3.51 per cent of all the emigrants. They have thus prevented 27,834 from going to the United States, have obviated the heartrending scenes witnessed in every case of deportation, and have saved these unfortunates from giving their last penny to the steamship companies, who would have had to bring them back to their native lands, penniless and homeless. When to this is added that, owing to the overcrowding in the steerage on every emigrant steamer, there are all the conditions favoring the transmission of trachoma and favus, it must be acknowledged that the Marine-Hospital Service has prevented thousands of emigrants from being infected with these dangerous and loathsome diseases.

After a thorough study of the methods applied to prevent the embarkation of diseased aliens for the United States, I have come to the conclusion that Naples is the only port where it is done conscientiously and honestly and with one view in mind, viz, the preventing of diseased aliens from reaching our ports. In all the other ports the steamship companies' physicians are in the main only looking for one thing—what aliens, though apparently or actually diseased, have a chance to pass the examination of the marine-hospital surgeons in America. At some ports the physicians are taking desperate chances and claim that they meet with success. I can state that my observations have convinced me that it is imperative that marine-hospital surgeons should be stationed at all the principal ports in Europe. Contagious disease could be kept from our shores and many healthy emigrants could be saved from infection while crossing the Atlantic by such a procedure, while the steamship companies ought to welcome it, because they would be spared the trouble and expense of carrying rejected aliens back to their native homes.

*   *   *   *   *   *   *

After a careful study of the emigration question in eastern and southern Europe, I feel called upon to report that the steamship companies can prevent the embarkation of undesirable emigrants for the United States. In fact they are preventing it to a certain extent and deserve commendation for the good work they are doing. There are, however, a few improvements in this work which I venture to suggest:

First. The steamship companies ought to be made to understand that they must not permit their physicians to apply medical treatment to any aliens affected with trachoma. This would do away with the "patching" up of diseased aliens, and thus preparing them for admission. * * *

Second. The representatives of the steamship companies at the German "control stations" should discontinue the practice of compelling emigrants to buy tickets for the United States when the aliens state that their destination is England or some other country. This fact has repeatedly been investigated by reporters of German newspapers, and details have been published. The steamship companies, it is true, have always denied that such is the fact, but I personally witnessed such cases while visiting these "control stations." The agents also have not denied it when I asked them about it. The only excuse they offer is that most of the aliens who claim that they intend to settle in England are "liars;" that in reality they intend to procure steamship tickets for America from non-German lines. This is no excuse for the agents, with the assistance of the police, compelling these unfortunates to buy tickets for America. Many honestly intend to settle in England, and there is no reason for coercing them to change their minds and go to the United States.

Third. The chief evil is the so-called "runner." It is he who goes around in eastern and southern Europe from city to city and from village to village telling fairy tales about the prosperity of many immigrants in America and the opportunities offered by the United States for aliens. The runner does not know of anyone who is undesirable; he claims to be all powerful, that he has representatives in every port who can "open the door" of America to anyone. It is he who induces many a diseased person to attempt the journey, and it is also he and his associates who do their best to have undesirables admitted. The steamship companies, as a rule, do not deal with these runners directly and disclaim all responsibility for their nefarious practices. But the official agents of the steamship companies do pay their runners commissions for every emigrant referred to them. I have especially studied this problem along the borders of Germany, Russia, and Austrian Galicia. Here most of the emigrants are smuggled across the frontier by these runners and robbed of the greater part of their cash possessions. When they arrive at the "control station," it is remarkable that most emigrants have cards with the address of a certain steamship ticket agent and the agent, on the other hand, has a list of all the individuals who were smuggled across the frontiers. When I asked one of these representatives how this was done, he told me that he paid "good commissions" to the runner on the other side of the frontier for each case. When steamship companies and their agents stop paying commissions to runners for emigrants referred to them, individuals only by their own initiative will attempt to go to the United States, and most of those of the classes which we consider undesirable will remain at their native homes.

Respectfully submitted.

MAURICE FISHBERG,
Immigrant Inspector.

Hon. FRANK P. SARGENT,
Commissioner-General of Immigration, Washington, D. C.

TRANSPORTATION LINES.

There have been two provisions in the statutes of the United States since March 3, 1891, and March 3, 1893, enacted for the purpose of restraining those engaged in bringing aliens to the United States within such bounds as to prevent a resort to means which would create an artificial or forced immigration. One of these prohibited other advertising in foreign countries by such carriers than the dates of sailings of their vessels and the cost and facilities of passage therein; the other required copies of the immigration laws, in the language of the country where passage is sold, to be posted conspicuously in all foreign ticket offices of the carriers, and even went so far as to require, under penalty for neglect or omission, a semiannual certificate that this provision has been regularly complied with. The facts are, as shown by the reports of those officers sent abroad for the purpose, referred to herein as well as last year, that the continent of Europe is dotted over with accredited agencies of the transportation lines, and they in turn have their subagents in every town and village, who resort to all the arts of persuasion known to such solicitors to induce aliens to purchase transportation to this country; that no fine has ever been imposed under the second provision, and that few aliens, except those who have been induced to come by promises of employment, exhibit the smallest knowledge of the immigration laws of this country.

In other words, the Bureau has to report that these two provisions, intended to restrain the transportation companies from seeking to foster immigration, are in its judgment practically inoperative, as has been shown elsewhere in discussing the inducements to the migration of aliens. In the competition for business these restraints provided by law have, either directly or through the system of commissions on the sale of transportation, been ignored, and the results are conspicuously evident in the enormous arrivals, aggregating a number in excess of 1,000,000 during the past year.

How far this fact consists with the repeatedly avowed desire and intent of the ocean carriers to observe the law in good faith Congress must determine, as it must also decide whether and how far additional means must be devised, through restraint of these vast instruments of capital, to lessen an influx of aliens into the United States, which it may well be feared constitutes a menace to the peace and good order of this country.

It is not reasonable to anticipate that if the great transportation lines do not respect the laws of this country their alien passengers will do so, nor can it be conceded that those aliens whose entrance to the United States is effected in spite of the law are desirable or even safe additions to our population.

More has been said on this subject in former reports of the Bureau, as well as herein, in treating of the subject of diseased alien immigrants, and a specific recommendation is made to hold the ocean carriers in check more effectively than is now done.

While fully realizing the commercial value to this country of those interests engaged in the business of carriers between this and foreign countries, it should be superfluous to say that there are other and larger stakes involved, and that if necessary to protect the United States from the dangers attendant upon unlimited immigration, adequate means should be resorted to by Congress to compel the observance by those interests both of the letter and the spirit of our laws.

It may not be improper to advert before concluding this subject to occasional instances of disregard by the masters or owners of vessels of provisions of the navigation laws intended to protect the health and comfort of passengers, although the administration of those laws is not within the purview of the Bureau's work, since it further confirms the opinion herein expressed. These infractions, one instance of which resulted during the year in the apparently needless death of several passengers on the voyage, are promptly reported to the appropriate administrative office.

NATURALIZATION AND DISTRIBUTION.

During the year indubitable evidence of fraud and carelessness in the matter of naturalizing aliens, or supplying them with evidence to sustain false claims to citizenship, has not been lacking, and the Bureau desires to reiterate the views expressed in its last report as to the necessity for such precautions being provided by law as will check, if not prevent, violations of the immigration laws by such means. As the subject of revising our naturalization laws has been referred to a special commission, it is unnecessary to enlarge upon this subject here, or to advert to the more serious ills that attend the lax system by which aliens, totally unfitted therefor either by duration of residence in this country, comprehension of and attachment to the principles of free representative government, or mental and moral qualifications, are clothed with the rights and privileges of citizenship, in many instances with as little ceremony or formality as attends the recording of a deed to property.

Again, the importance of undertaking to distribute aliens now congregating in our large cities to those parts of the United States where they can secure employment without displacing others by working for a less wage, and where the conditions of existence do not tend to the fostering of disease, depravity, and resistance to the social and political security of the country, is urged. The Bureau is not unmindful of the obstacles presented to the formation of a feasible plan for this purpose, but it submits that the matter is one of such importance as to demand the attention of the Government, both general and local. It is impossible to believe that a practical device can not be found, if not through the action of the Federal Government alone, then with the cooperation of the State and civic authorities. It has been pointed out that, so far as the overcrowding in city tenements is concerned, municipal ordinances in our large cities prescribing the amount of space which rapacious landlords should, under penalties sufficiently heavy to enforce obedience, be required to give each tenant, would go far toward attaining the object in view.

Whether such a plan could be brought into existence through the efforts of our General Government, or whether under any of its constitutional powers, express or implied, the Congress could itself legislate directly, upon sanitary or moral grounds, against the notorious practice of housing aliens with less regard for health and comfort than is shown in placing brute animals in pens, the Bureau is unprepared to say, even if an expression of its views upon the subject were necessary. It is, however, convinced that no feature of the immigration question so insistently demands public attention and effective action. The evil to be removed is one that is steadily and rapidly on the increase, and its removal will strike at the roots of fraudulent elections, poverty, disease, and crime in our large cities, and, on the other hand, largely supply that increasing demand for labor to develop the natural resources of our country.

As affording reasonable assurance of a check upon the continued growth of this evil too much encouragement can not be given to the reported efforts of certain railway companies to divert a portion of the tide of immigration to the Southern States.

It is impossible, in the opinion of the Bureau, to overestimate the importance of this subject as bearing upon the effect of immigration on the future welfare of this country.

ALIEN INMATES OF PENAL, REFORMATORY, AND CHARITABLE INSTITUTIONS.

There are given below three of the tables presented in the last report to show, as bearing upon the expulsion of aliens who have become public charges, the number in our various public institutions for mental or moral defects or because they are unable to support themselves. A careful consideration of these figures can not fail to suggest the wisdom of the restriction on immigration elsewhere suggested, as well as the desirability of giving relief from the burden of supporting such aliens by providing for their return to the countries whence they came.

[Attention is invited to explanation under the heading of "Chart 8" on page 106, which explanation also applies to the following tables.]

TABLE 1.—ALIENS DETAINED IN **PENAL, REFORMATORY,** AND **CHARITABLE INSTITUTIONS** OF THE UNITED STATES.

DETAILS, BY RACES, OF ALIENS DETAINED.

Subdivision of races.	Alien inmates.	Sex.		Age.		Cause.				Probable period of detention.			Jurisdiction of institution.			
		Males.	Females.	Under 21.	21 and over.	Criminals. Grave.	Criminals. Minor.	Insane.	Paupers.	Under 2 years.	2 years and over.	Life.	Federal.	State.	County.	Private.
African (black)	208	162	46	35	173	62	54	52	40	68	85	55	1	117	70	20
Armenian	59	52	7	8	51	6	4	24	25	22	13	24		37	14	8
Bohemian and Moravian (Czech)	406	250	156	39	367	20	28	251	107	79	76	251	2	224	155	25
Bulgarian, Servian, and Montenegrin	7	7		2	5	1	2	3	1	2	2	3		4	3	
Chinese	670	659	11	21	649	207	108	317	38	164	174	332	5	460	197	8
Croatian and Slovenian	129	122	7	21	108	10	36	27	56	86	15	28		36	68	25
Cuban	59	55	4	14	45	12	9	26	12	17	18	24		39	10	10
Dalmatian, Bosnian, and Herzegovinian	5	5			5		1	2	2	3		2		2	1	2
Dutch and Flemish	183	148	35	18	165	21	27	81	54	41	31	111	12	106	64	1
East Indian	23	19	4	1	22	5		16	2	3	5	15		15	8	
English	4,248	2,883	1,365	413	3,835	420	697	1,884	1,247	990	879	2,379	94	2,548	1,237	369
Finnish	383	320	63	26	357	40	67	198	78	112	80	191	4	252	103	24
French	1,948	1,421	527	281	1,667	197	421	823	507	469	409	1,070	18	1,170	615	145
German	9,050	6,024	3,026	673	8,377	587	706	5,041	2,716	1,467	1,442	6,141	222	4,826	3,314	688
Greek	103	98	5	26	77	19	25	21	38	54	33	16	20	35	35	13
Hebrew	2,765	1,669	1,096	1,206	1,559	170	389	935	1,271	640	1,058	1,067	2	1,169	715	879
Irish	11,980	5,423	6,557	442	11,538	283	1,155	6,137	4,405	2,434	1,116	8,430	260	6,365	3,950	1,405
Italian	3,266	2,802	464	863	2,403	755	563	733	1,215	1,147	1,300	819	22	1,588	950	706
Japanese	229	210	19	16	213	96	28	42	63	90	46	93	3	122	55	49
Korean	4	4			4			4		4			2	1		1
Lithuanian	196	177	19	19	177	21	54	20	101	135	26	35	1	43	115	37
Magyar	507	379	128	104	403	67	95	180	165	180	149	178	6	223	184	94
Mexican	908	832	76	114	794	495	205	94	114	269	462	177	4	554	301	49
Pacific Islander	1	1			1			1				1		1		
Polish	2,064	1,601	463	317	1,747	227	393	667	777	826	444	794	15	854	934	261
Portuguese	188	139	44	20	163	16	19	91	57	56	51	96	6	118	39	25
Roumanian	52	45	7	16	36	9	12	8	23	26	17	9		24	15	13
Russian	324	253	71	50	274	47	53	154	70	102	118	104	7	170	111	36
Ruthenian (Russniak)	20	20		1	19		2	6	12	14	3	3		4	10	6
Scandinavian (Norwegians, Danes, and Swedes)	3,125	2,139	986	165	2,960	155	238	2,039	693	582	491	2,052	27	2,008	927	163
Scotch	903	603	300	83	820	80	149	340	334	246	136	521	5	472	319	107
Slovak	438	361	77	52	386	29	98	95	216	253	60	125		128	219	91
Spanish	151	130	21	28	123	26	14	58	53	49	44	58	5	67	52	27
Spanish-American	42	38	4	6	36	7	18	10	7	4	12	26		18	15	9
Syrian	107	74	33	64	43	8	18	8	73	38	59	10		25	26	56

Turkish	38	35	3	12	26	6	7	16	9	8	15	15	1	28	5	4
Welsh	175	121	54	9	166	15	13	78	69	36	20	119	3	90	67	15
West Indian	26	18	8	8	18	5	3	6	12	12	9	5		11	7	8
Total	44,985	29,299	15,686	5,173	39,812	4,124	5,701	20,485	14,675	10,731	8,928	25,381	701	23,975	14,918	5,391

CHARACTER OF INSTITUTION.

Charitable	15,396	9,391	6,005	2,992	12,404			721		4,832	2,357	8,207		1,583	8,474	5,339
Insane	19,764	10,888	8,876	283	19,481			19,764	14,675	1,358	1,621	16,785	660	17,133	1,919	52
Penal	9,825	9,020	805	1,898	7,927					4,541	4,945	389	41	5,259	4,525	
All institutions	44,985	29,299	15,686	5,173	39,812	4,124	5,701	20,485	14,675	10,731	8,928	25,381	701	23,975	14,918	5,391

LENGTH OF TIME IN THE UNITED STATES.

Character of institution.	1 year.	2 years.	3 years.	4 and 5 years.	6 to 10 years.	11 to 20 years.	21 to 30 years.	31 to 40 years.	Over 40 years.
	Per cent.	Per cent.	Per cent.	Per cent.	Per cent.	Per cent.	Per cent.	Per cent.	Per cent.
Charitable			4	7	8	20	15	16	18
Insane	1	1	2	5	12	35	22	14	8
Penal	5	5	6	13	20	33	12	5	1
All institutions	5	4	4	8	13	28	16	12	10

PORTS OF LANDING.

Port.	Per cent.	Port.	Per cent.	Port.	Per cent.
New York	71	Baltimore	3	Canadian ports	8
Boston	7	San Francisco	2	All other ports	5
Philadelphia	4				

NUMBER AND **PROPORTION** OF ALIEN INMATES OF EACH CLASS OF INSTITUTION AND ALL INSTITUTIONS, **BELONGING TO EACH RACIAL DIVISION.**

Subdivision of race.	Class of institution.							
	Charitable.		Insane.		Penal.		All.	
	Number.	Per cent.	Number.	Per cent.	Number.	Per cent.	Number.	Per cent.
African (black)	43	$\frac{3}{10}$	49	$\frac{3}{10}$	116	$1\frac{2}{10}$	208	$\frac{4}{10}$
Armenian	25	$\frac{2}{10}$	24	$\frac{1}{10}$	10	$\frac{1}{10}$	59	$\frac{1}{10}$
Bohemian and Moravian (Czech)	116	$\frac{7}{10}$	242	$1\frac{2}{10}$	48	$\frac{5}{10}$	406	$\frac{9}{10}$
Bulgarian, Servian, and Montenegrin	1	$\frac{1}{100}$	3	$\frac{1}{100}$	3	$\frac{3}{100}$	7	$\frac{1}{100}$
Chinese	40	$\frac{3}{10}$	315	$1\frac{6}{10}$	315	$3\frac{2}{10}$	670	$1\frac{5}{10}$
Croatian and Slovenian	60	$\frac{4}{10}$	23	$\frac{1}{10}$	46	$\frac{5}{10}$	129	$\frac{3}{10}$
Cuban	12	$\frac{8}{100}$	26	$\frac{1}{10}$	21	$\frac{2}{10}$	59	$\frac{1}{10}$
Dalmatian, Bosnian, and Herzegovinian	2	$\frac{1}{100}$	2	$\frac{1}{100}$	1	$\frac{1}{100}$	5	$\frac{1}{100}$
Dutch and Flemish	57	$\frac{4}{10}$	78	$\frac{4}{10}$	48	$\frac{5}{10}$	183	$\frac{4}{10}$
East Indian	2	$\frac{1}{100}$	16	$\frac{8}{100}$	5	$\frac{5}{100}$	23	$\frac{5}{100}$
English	1,309	$8\frac{5}{10}$	1,822	9	1,117	11	4,248	9
Finnish	80	$\frac{5}{10}$	196	1	107	$1\frac{1}{10}$	383	$\frac{8}{10}$
French	535	$3\frac{5}{10}$	795	4	618	6	1,948	$4\frac{3}{10}$
German	2,949	19	4,808	24	1,293	13	9,050	20
Greek	38	$\frac{2}{10}$	21	1	44	$\frac{5}{10}$	103	$\frac{2}{10}$
Hebrew	1,274	8	932	5	559	6	2,765	6
Irish	4,599	30	5,943	30	1,438	15	11,980	27
Italian	1,230	8	718	$3\frac{6}{10}$	1,318	$13\frac{4}{10}$	3,266	$7\frac{3}{10}$
Japanese	63	$\frac{4}{10}$	42	$\frac{2}{10}$	124	$1\frac{2}{10}$	229	$\frac{5}{10}$
Korean	1	$\frac{1}{100}$	1	$\frac{1}{100}$	2	$\frac{2}{100}$	4	$\frac{1}{100}$
Lithuanian	104	$\frac{7}{10}$	17	$\frac{9}{100}$	75	$\frac{8}{10}$	196	$\frac{4}{10}$
Magyar	177	1	169	$\frac{9}{10}$	162	$1\frac{6}{10}$	507	1
Mexican	117	$\frac{8}{10}$	90	$\frac{5}{10}$	700	7	908	2
Pacific Islander			1	$\frac{1}{100}$	1		1	
Polish	839	$5\frac{5}{10}$	605	3	620	6	2,064	5
Portuguese	57	$\frac{4}{10}$	91	$\frac{5}{10}$	35	$\frac{4}{10}$	183	$\frac{4}{10}$
Roumanian	23	$\frac{1}{100}$	8	$\frac{4}{100}$	21	$\frac{2}{10}$	52	$\frac{1}{10}$
Russian	78	$\frac{5}{10}$	146	$\frac{7}{10}$	100	1	324	$1\frac{1}{10}$
Ruthenian (Russniak)	13	$\frac{8}{100}$	5	$\frac{3}{100}$	2	$\frac{2}{100}$	20	$\frac{4}{100}$
Scandinavian (Norwegians, Danes, and Swedes)	747	5	1,985	10	393	4	3,125	7
Scotch	342	2	332	$1\frac{7}{10}$	229	$2\frac{3}{10}$	903	2
Slovak	224	$1\frac{5}{10}$	86	$\frac{4}{10}$	128	$1\frac{3}{10}$	438	1
Spanish	54	$\frac{3}{10}$	58	$\frac{2}{10}$	39	$\frac{4}{10}$	151	$\frac{3}{10}$
Spanish-American	19	$\frac{1}{100}$	10	$\frac{5}{100}$	13	$\frac{1}{10}$	42	$\frac{1}{10}$
Syrian	73	$\frac{5}{10}$	8	$\frac{4}{100}$	26	$\frac{3}{10}$	107	$\frac{2}{10}$
Turkish	9	$\frac{6}{100}$	16	$\frac{8}{100}$	13	$\frac{1}{10}$	38	$\frac{8}{100}$
Welsh	72	$\frac{5}{10}$	75	$\frac{4}{10}$	28	$\frac{3}{10}$	175	$\frac{4}{10}$
West Indian	12	$\frac{8}{100}$	6	$\frac{3}{100}$	8	$\frac{8}{100}$	26	$\frac{6}{100}$
Total	15,396	100	19,764	100	9,825	100	44,985	100

ALL ALIENS IN PENAL, REFORMATORY, AND CHARITABLE INSTITUTIONS OF EACH SECTION OF COUNTRY, BY GRAND DIVISION OF RACE, SHOWING THE PER CENT OF ALIEN INMATES OF EACH SECTION BELONGING TO EACH **RACIAL GRAND DIVISION.**

Grand division of race.a	North Atlantic section.		South Atlantic section.		North Central section.		South Central section.		Western section.		Hawaii.		Porto Rico.		Total.	
	Number.	Per cent.	Number.	Per cent.	Number.	Per cent.	Number.	Per cent.	Number.	Per cent.	Number.	Per cent.	Number.	Per cent.	Number.	Per cent.
Teutonic	7,750	28	926	49	5,719	63	403	32	2,177	43	11	4	3	9	16,989	38
Keltic	11,007	40	649	34	1,858	20	334	26	1,156	23	1	.....	1	3	15,006	33
Slavic	4,895	18	160	8	1,079	12	65	5	202	4	4	1½	1	3	6,406	14
Iberic	2,898	11	97	5	268	3	69	5	431	8	31	11	16	45	3,810	9
Mongolic	126	½	4	.....	20	.....	2	.....	546	11	228	81	1	3	927	2
All others	625	2½	73	4	138	2	409	32	582	11	7	2½	13	37	1,847	4
Total	27,301	100	1,909	100	9,082	100	1,282	100	5,094	100	282	100	35	100	44,985	100

a See page 103 for race classification.

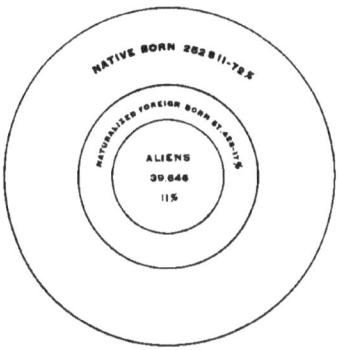

IMMIGRATION THROUGH CANADA.

The steady increase in immigration through the Dominion of Canada is shown by the following table covering the reports for the past five years:

Fiscal year ended June 30—

1901	25, 220
1902	29, 199
1903	35, 920
1904	30, 374
1905	44, 214

So different are the conditions under which the immigration laws are administered at seaports of the United States from those which prevail at the ports of Canada, and so certain does it appear that this indirect mode of migrating to this country will continue, that the Bureau considers it indispensable to a correct understanding of the subject to make an exception to the general rule as to publishing reports of its officers, and includes herein the report of Commissioner Clark, who has charge of the entire Canadian border:

OFFICE OF COMMISSIONER OF IMMIGRATION,
Montreal, Canada, July 1, 1905.

SIR: I have the honor to invite the attention of the Bureau to the subjoined report relative to immigration to the United States from Europe via Canadian ocean ports, and from Canada via border ports, for the fiscal year ended June 30, 1905.

IMMIGRATION TO CANADA.

Perhaps no other government that we might name is at present devoting the time, thought, and money to the subject of increase of population that is now being contributed by the Dominion government with a view to inducing immigration to Canada.

It may very properly be added, in connection with the immigration policy of the Canadian authorities, that nothing savors of the spasmodic or temporary, for from the substantial and commodious landing quarters erected at each of the important seaports in Canada to the well-equipped hospitals for the treatment of those arriving aliens who do not measure up to the physical requirements at the time of disembarkation, one sees unmistakable evidences of the fact that to intending settlers Canada is preparing to extend a welcome for some years to come.

There are at the present time, approximately, 48 steamships engaged in the immigrant carrying business to the ports of Canada. Recent steps taken by the various Canadian steamship lines to provide increased accommodations for immigrants would indicate the faith of the owners in the claim that prospective immigration to Canada, and through Canada to the United States, affords a field for investment of which they should avail themselves.

During the fiscal year which this report is intended to cover the Allan Line Company has added to its fleet the two new steamships *Victorian* and *Virginian*, the first of the turbine-engine pattern to enter the trans-Atlantic service, and the Canadian Pacific Railway Atlantic Steamship Company is about to add to its list of steamships now in commission two new liners of the most modern build.

The Donaldson Line Company, one of the old established freight lines, has embarked in the passenger business by putting into commission for the Glasgow-Canada trade the steamship *Athenia,* and added thereto a service has been established between Mexico and Canadian points, touching at Havana en route, so that we may reasonably expect to find in the near future immigrants seeking landing in Canada from Mexico and South American countries.

For the fiscal year ended June 30, 1904, the amount appropriated by the Dominion government on account of immigration was $745,229.26, and for the fiscal year ended June 30, 1905, the amount was increased to $972,426.04.

As to the results attained by the expenditure of the above sums, the total immigration to Canada for 1904 was 130,331, and for the fiscal year just ended, 146,266. For the year ended June 30, 1905, through the courtesy of the honorable superintendent of immigration at Ottawa, I am able to inform the Bureau that of the total arrivals in Canada 102,048 came via Atlantic ports, 675 via Pacific ports, and 45,543 from the friendly Republic lying south of the Dominion.

The above does not, of course, include arrivals at Canadian ports manifested to United States destinations, and examined under the laws controlling immigration to the United States. It is with regard to the latter, and in addition to the large number of aliens originally ticketed to points in Canada, but who subsequently by the various avenues of entrance along the Canadian boundary sought access to the United States that this report has to deal.

IMMIGRATION THROUGH AND FROM CANADA TO THE UNITED STATES.

The control of immigration to the United States through Canada having been arranged for by an agreement between Canadian steamship and transportation lines and our Government, in presenting a report concerning the entrance of aliens to the United States by this route it has been deemed important, as in the past, to show complete data as to numbers, nationalities, causes for rejections, etc., regarding those coming within the purview of said agreement, and, in addition, similar data concerning those whose length of residence in Canada precludes their consideration under other authority than that contained in the general immigration laws and regulations.

In order to follow out this plan of report it is found necessary to divide the aliens entering the United States during the fiscal year just ended into three separate classes, to wit:

First. Aliens arriving at Canadian ocean ports manifested to United States destinations.

Second. Aliens who arrived at Canadian ocean ports and, having remained in Canada less than one year, applied for admission at the border, and were examined under the terms of Department Circular 97.

Third. Aliens who applied at the border for admission, having resided in Canada for a period of more than one year.

The following table (No. 1) shows total arrivals at Canada-Atlantic ports of aliens manifested to the United States and the action taken regarding them.

TABLE 1.—ALIENS DESTINED TO UNITED STATES LANDED AT CANADIAN ATLANTIC PORTS BY STEAMSHIP LINES NAMED, YEAR ENDED JUNE 30, 1905.

Steamship lines.	Examined.	Admitted on primary examination.	Admitted after being temporarily detained.	Admitted after special inquiry.	Total admitted.	Total debarred.	Total deported.	Debarred and remained in Canada.	Pending.	Percentage debarred.
Allan Line	6,587	5,645	662	268	6,475	100	52	48	12	1.51
Canadian Pacific Railway Atlantic Line	4,469	3,836	452	112	4,400	45	37	8	14	1.01
Canadian Lines (Limited)	103	51	29	22	102	1	1			.97
Dominion Line	1,667	1,365	211	67	1,643	15	13	2	9	.90
Donaldson Line	65	28	14	1	43	22	20	2	....	33.84
Total	12,881	10,825	1,368	470	12,663	183	123	60	35	......

Percentage debarred, 1.42.

Table No. 2 shows the total number of aliens applying at the border for admission to the United States, and examined by boards of special inquiry, within one year from date of arrival at a Canadian ocean port, and in Table No. 3 is shown the number of aliens examined by border boards of special inquiry, said aliens having resided in Canada for periods in excess of one year.

Following in regular order may be found Table No. 4, giving the stations at which aliens reported in Tables No. 2 and No. 3 were examined, and showing the number rejected at each station by races, and causes therefor, the recapitulation table giving the rejections by races and causes at all border stations where there are boards of special inquiry.

Table No. 5 is inserted to show the total number of aliens denied admission at border stations where there are no boards of special inquiry; and it is deemed worthy of comment that of the 524 rejected because of "No certificate," but 152 returned for "payment of head tax, examination, and certificate," as per the terms of Department Circular 97, and it does not seem unreasonable to presume that those failing to return were of the class regarded by the Bureau as undesirable.

TABLE 2.—ALIENS IN CANADA LESS THAN ONE YEAR EXAMINED BY BORDER BOARDS OF SPECIAL INQUIRY UNDER THE PROVISIONS OF DEPARTMENT CIRCULAR NO. 97, SHOWING STEAMSHIP LINES BRINGING THEM, YEAR ENDED JUNE 30, 1905.

Steamship lines.	Admitted.	Rejected.	Pending.
Allan Line	3,738	215	4
Canadian Pacific Atlantic Line	2,195	169	22
Canadian Lines (Limited)	343	65	....
Dominion Line	1,631	101	8
Donaldson Line	21	4	1
Hamburg Line	104	2	....
Miscellaneous	485	33	1

Percentage debarred, 6.44.

TABLE 3.—ALIENS IN CANADA MORE THAN ONE YEAR EXAMINED BY BORDER BOARDS OF SPECIAL INQUIRY UNDER THE PROVISIONS OF DEPARTMENT CIRCULAR NO. 43, YEAR ENDED JUNE 30, 1905.

Admitted 19,308
Rejected 749
Pending 19

Percentage debarred, 3.73.

TABLE 4.—REJECTIONS, BY CAUSES AND RACES, OF ALIENS EXAMINED BY BORDER BOARDS OF SPECIAL INQUIRY, YEAR ENDED JUNE 30, 1905.

Race.	Assisted immigrants.	Convicted of crime.	Contract laborers.	Likely to become public charges.	To prevent separation of family.	Prostitutes.	Idiots.	Insane.	Favus.	Trachoma.	Other debarring diseases.	Total.
Armenian				3						14	1	18
Bohemian				1								1
Croatian				5						19	2	26
Dalmatian				9							2	11
Dutch and Flemish			2	6						3		11
English			36	111			2			9	4	162
Finnish			2	15						17	14	48
French			9	2	3	1					1	16
German			6	22	4					7	4	43
Greek		1	7	2						12	4	26
Hebrew	4		10	87	7	1		1	19	63	6	198
Irish			5	11						1	3	20
Italian (north)			4		1					2		7
Italian (south)			65	67	3		1		8	102	11	257
Japanese			1	2						1		4
Lithuanian				2						10		12
Magyar			10	4						74	5	93
Mexican				2								2
Moravian				1								1
Polish	2		4	39				1	1	63	9	119
Russian			2	10						7	1	20
Roumanian				7						6		13
Ruthenian			2	6								8
Scotch			9	28	4					1	2	44
Slovak			2	7	1					26	2	38
Syrian			6	18	6				1	33	3	67
Scandinavian			8	33	7			1		12	5	66
Turkish				2								2
Welsh			3	1						1		5
West Indian			1	1								2
Canadian citizens		2	138	157	4	10	5	8		9	3	336
Total	6	3	332	661	40	12	8	11	29	492	82	1,676

TABLE 5.—REJECTIONS AT BORDER STATIONS HAVING NO BOARDS OF SPECIAL INQUIRY, YEAR ENDED JUNE 30, 1905.

Station.	No certificate.	Suspected cause.							Total.
		Contract laborers.	Likely to become public charges.	Prostitutes.	Idiots.	Insane.	Favus.	Other debarring diseases.	
Alburg, Vt	28								28
Blaine, Wash. a	19		7						26
Cape Vincent, N. Y	27	1	6			2			36
Charlotte, N. Y		1							1
Cornwall, Ontario	2								2
Deloraine, Manitoba	12								12
Fort Francis, Ontario	8		2					1	11
Gateway, Mont	9			1					10
Malone, N. Y	9								9
Morristown, N. Y	17		13						30
Neche, N. Dak	135	3	3					2	143
North Stratford, N. H	18	3	17						38
Newport, Vt	30	1	12		1		1		45
Oswego, N. Y	2		1						3
Ogdensburg, N. Y	17	4	44						65
Pembina, N. Dak	78	11	18						107
Rouses Point, N. Y	64								64
Rainy River, Ontario	22	2	4	3					31
Warroad, Minn	11		2						13
St. Albans, Vt	9		7						16
Swanton, Vt	7	5	3						15
Total	524	31	139	4	1	2	1	3	705

a Board organized October, 1904.

Subsequently admitted by boards of special inquiry... 152
Actual rejections... 553

Departmental instructions dated May 10, 1904 (circular 43), direct that "citizens of Canada and Newfoundland should be examined under the immigration laws as to their right to enter the United States, but should not be manifested and reported for statistical purposes, and no head tax should be collected." It will be understood, therefore, by those studying the foregoing tables that they do not include citizens of Canada or Newfoundland who, as in previous years, no doubt in large numbers during the period covered by this report migrated to the United States.

While the work of supplying the Bureau with such data would naturally augment the present duties of your border officers, yet a report showing the number of aliens entering the United States through and from Canada must remain incomplete unless data concerning the Canadian citizen class be shown. Under present regulations the examination of citizens of Canada and Newfoundland, under the immigration laws, as to their right to enter the United States is required, and manifesting of Canadian citizens intending to settle in the United States, for statistical purposes, would offer little or no annoyance to passengers in ordinary travel.

Similar data are being collected by the Dominion government with regard to settlers from the United States, and by recording for statistical purposes Canadian citizens who contemplate residence in the great Republic the Bureau would be in a position to determine to what extent immigration to Canada is likely to affect our own population.

To form an estimate as to the actual number of Canadians crossing the border into the United States each year, one has but to reflect upon the constant emigration of native Canadians to the New England cities and other large centers of population adjacent to the northern boundary line.

In connection with the above phase of the work in this jurisdiction, from personal observation I am convinced that the recent census taken in the United States will demonstrate, to the surprise of many, that the trend of immigration is not altogether toward the north.

While the above carefully prepared tables show the total rejections for the year, we have yet to take cognizance of a considerable number of aliens, which, to properly classify, must be added to those who were excluded after examination.

The Bureau has ruled that guaranty of payment of head tax is prerequisite to examination, and during the fiscal year now being considered a total of 1,734 aliens sought admission to the United States at the various border stations for whom the transportation lines carrying them refused to guarantee payment of head tax. These aliens were therefore classed as "not properly presented for examination," and were returned to Canada.

It may be said that nearly every applicant for admission of the class just mentioned was totally without funds, and examination could only have resulted in exclusion as persons likely to become public charges; and while aliens of the class now being considered do not appear in the record of those examined, yet it seems perfectly proper that they should be added to the list of those rejected, and are considered from that viewpoint in the following table (No. 6) summarizing the year's work.

TABLE 6.—SUMMARY OF WORK PERFORMED UNDER THE MONTREAL OFFICE, YEAR ENDED JUNE 30, 1905.

	Examined.	Admitted.	Debarred.	Pending.	Per cent debarred.
Arrivals at Canadian Atlantic ports manifested under Department Circular No. 97...	12,881	12,663	183	35	1.42
Manifested by border boards of special inquiry under Department Circular No. 97...	9,142	8,517	589	36	6.44
Manifested by border boards of special inquiry under Department Circular No. 43...	20,076	19,308	749	19	3.73
Total manifested.......................	42,099	40,488	1,521	90	....
Rejected at stations having no boards of special inquiry..............................	553	....	553	....	....
Aliens not properly presented for examination, hence debarred.....................	....	....	1,734	....	....
Grand total............................	42,652	40,488	3,808	90	a 8.92

a Total percentage debarred.

Head tax accruing from aliens examined... $85,304.00
Money shown by aliens admitted.. 1,905,211.00
Amount per capita.. 47.05

PHYSICAL CONDITION OF ALIENS REPORTED ABOVE.

Comparison of the report herewith submitted with that of the year preceding will show that the proportion of aliens certified on account of disease is practically the same for the two years, and the fact that the class reported in Table No. 2—aliens in Canada less than one year—is still producing five times the number of diseased and undesirables found in the class manifested to United States destinations and examined at the port of disembarkation suggests the wisdom of continuing the present careful inspection at the border.

It will be noted that of the aliens who had been in Canada less than one year a total of 603 were denied admission at the border because of loathsome or dangerous contagious diseases, and as a large proportion of the above class proceeded to the border directly from the steamship upon which they arrived, this office has constantly insisted that these aliens be registered in United States manifests, thus enabling us to enforce examination at the port of landing and to arrange for deportation of all aliens suffering from communicable diseases.

The steamship companies have shown a willingness to enforce proper manifesting, yet, despite all our efforts, either through the influence of unscrupulous booking agents in Europe, or with a view to availing themselves of the slight.y cheaper rate offered by the Canadian lines, aliens destined to the United States continue to book to points in Canada, thus, as regards deportation, in cases where disease is certified, defeating the requirements of the United States immigration laws.

The 603 diseased aliens referred to above were returned to Canada, it being understood by this office that the deportation of an alien who has been regularly landed in Canada is impracticable under the Dominion immigration act.

The Dominion government has greatly improved its immigration service in many ways, yet our record of disease among aliens who have been in Canada less than one year shows either that there is still room for improvement or that there exists a disparity between the medical inspection of the Dominion and United States examiners not easily accounted for by the unprofessional.

Should the Dominion authorities concede the diagnosing of the Bureau's medical examiners to be reliable, and should there exist a desire to relieve Canada of the presence of so many contagiously diseased aliens, much may be accomplished by united action in the direction of insisting that all aliens be properly manifested before disembarkation.

The reports of our medical examiners at Quebec and Montreal are respectfully submitted, showing not only the number of aliens who were contagiously diseased, but also those having minor defects, and for the future a similar report will be filed from each station in this jurisdiction.

OFFICE OF COMMISSIONER OF IMMIGRATION,
Montreal, Canada, June 30, 1905.

SIR: I have the honor to submit my report as medical officer in charge of the medical division at Montreal, Canada, for the fiscal year ended June 30, 1905. During this period I issued 7,461 medical certificates, of which number I certified to 134 cases of loathsome and dangerous contagious diseases.

*   *   *   *   *   *   *

There were held for observation 178 cases, of which the following disposition was made:

Eventually granted certificates of health _____ 71
Eventually certified to disease_____ 29
Failed to reappear for examination _____ 78
                                                                      ———
    Total observation_____ 178

Respectfully,   JAMES BARCLAY,
                                              United States Medical Examiner.
Hon. JOHN H. CLARK,
    Commissioner of Immigration, Montreal, Canada.

Doctor Kerr reports that at the end of the fiscal year 1904 there were 32 cases of diseased aliens remaining on hand at the Quebec and St. John stations, which, with the 285 certified for various diseases during the year 1905, made a total of 317, which are accounted for in the following manner: Released by boards of special inquiry, 122; released by Canadian authorities, 19; released as recovered, 84; escaped, 3; died, 1; deported, 80; and remaining under treatment at close of year, 8.

VIOLATIONS OF THE IMMIGRATION LAWS.

During the fiscal year of 1905 officers in this jurisdiction deported under Department warrants a total of 46 aliens, who had become public charges within two years from date of arrival in the United States. Of the above number 20 were deported from New York, 8 from Canadian ports, and 18 were deported to Canada.

Your officers connected with the border force have rendered splendid service during the past year by showing their ability to cope with those who would set our laws at defiance by aiding inadmissibles to effect surreptitious entry to the United States.

Attempts at lawbreaking have been numerous, but your officers have been found ready for almost every emergency, and arrests have been made and punishment administered in each case, including two very important contract-labor cases at Eastport and Calais, Me., respectively, where the court imposed a fine of $1,000 in each instance.

I am sure the Bureau will appreciate that the work of following the operations of cunning smugglers means long hours of duty for those officers engaged in the border service, and I regard it as being greatly to the credit of the officers mentioned that in each case where arrest was thought advisable a conviction has been secured.

EXTENSION OF THE JURISDICTION OF THE MONTREAL OFFICE.

By an order dated February 20, 1905, the Bureau was pleased to extend the jurisdiction of the Montreal office to include the ports of Vancouver and Victoria, British Columbia, which order became operative March 1, 1905. Investigation disclosed the fact that the work of inspection at these two ports was not being conducted in accordance with methods employed elsewhere in the Bureau's service and a number of changes was deemed necessary.

Inasmuch as the corps of officers on duty at Vancouver and Victoria is competent and conscientious, I can see no reason why the Bureau may not expect to find before the expiration of many months that matters in the western end of this jurisdiction are working satisfactorily, and that the immigration laws are being enforced under the rules governing the service at other important ports of landing.

In the foregoing tables the alien arrivals at the two western ports named are not taken into consideration, owing to the fact that prior to March 1, 1905, manifests containing data concerning aliens arriving at Vancouver and Victoria were sent direct to the Bureau of the Census for compilation; hence this office is not in a position to report correctly for the whole year.

In submitting Table No. 8, however, correct figures for the last four months of 1905 are given, and for the eight months preceding the figures given will at least approximate completeness, and for correctness comparisons may be made with records now on file at the Bureau of the Census.

Steps have been taken to enable this Office for the current year to supply the Bureau with detailed information as to the immigration to the United States from trans-Pacific ports via Vancouver and Victoria, the table now submitted showing in the number arriving and the percentage of aliens debarred that the ports named represent an important branch of the Bureau's service.

TABLE 8.—ALIENS ARRIVING AT VANCOUVER AND VICTORIA MANIFESTED TO UNITED STATES FOR THE YEAR ENDED JUNE 30, 1905, SHOWING DISPOSITION OF SAME.

Month.	Examined.	Admitted.	Debarred.	Loathsome or dangerous contagious diseases.	Likely to become public charges.	Contract laborers.	Prostitutes.	Epileptic.
1904.								
July	539	505	34	13	20	1	......	......
August..............................	536	516	20	3	16	1	......	......
September	504	474	30	8	20	2	......	......
October..............................	435	415	20	4	13	3	......	......
November	428	421	7	1	6	......	......	......
December..............................	277	270	7	2	5	......	......	......
1905.								
January..............................	144	136	8	3	3	1	1	......
February	184	178	6	2	2	1	1	......
March	308	308	......	......	......	......	......	......
April..............................	316	316	......	......	......	......	......	......
May..............................	591	569	22	14	5	2	......	1
June	370	352	18	16	2	1	......	......
Total..............................	4,632	4,460	172	65	92	12	2	1

RECOMMENDATIONS.

In his annual report for the fiscal year ended June 30, 1903, Commissioner Watchorn made use of the following:

"Special stress must be laid on the recommendation that none but young, active, strong, and robust men should be assigned to duty on the frontier, and they should be selected with a view to putting none but men of good judgment in these places of unusual importance and responsibility."

The experiences of the two years intervening compel me to lend the strongest possible approval to the above recommendation of my predecessor.

While the tables submitted in this report show that for the fiscal year of 1905 a total of 48,718 aliens sought access to the United States from Canada, yet, to the ordinary reader, they must prove almost wholly inadequate as affording a proper understanding of the difficulties surmounted in manifesting, in accordance with the requirements of the law, for statistical and other purposes, this large number of aliens.

This office has active accounts with no less than forty-five corporations doing a passenger-transportation business across the northern boundary, between the Atlantic and Pacific oceans, and from incomplete reports now to hand, by trains, trolleys, ferry, and lake boats, more than 6,000,000 passengers entered the United States from Canada last year.

The 48,718 aliens were selected from the above millions, the immigration laws having no application to the balance, and this difficult task was performed without inconvenience to the traveling public or interference with the time schedules of train or boat service.

I am glad to assure the Bureau that the latter conditions exist even at Niagara Falls, where thousands of passengers enter the United States every twenty-four hours, which heavy travel is constantly taken advantage of by large numbers of aliens who seek access to the United States in evasion of inspection, among the latter being many who have previously been excluded.

No less than 150,000 passengers crossed the border into the United States at Niagara Falls during June last, from which number our officers detained 694 of the taxable class, and whose examination before a board of special inquiry was necessary under the law.

As regards tact, judgment, courtesy, ability to endure long hours of service, a thorough knowledge of the law and how to apply it quickly, in order that traffic may not be interfered with, I question whether there is any other position in the Government service more exacting than that of immigrant inspector in the border service, and I can not too strongly urge that only officers possessing the qualifications named above be assigned to duty in this jurisdiction.

On February 17, 1905, the writer was honored by promotion to succeed Mr. Robert Watchorn as commissioner of immigration for Canada. Since assuming charge in this jurisdiction, believing such action would meet the commendation of the Department, effort has been made to conduct the work of the Bureau along lines laid down by Mr. Watchorn, with only such changes as the exigencies of the service or continued experience might suggest.

Between the Dominion government, Canadian steamship and transportation lines, and this office, relations of the most cordial character continue to exist, this happy condition in no small measure being due, in the opinion of the writer, to the growing feeling among citizens of Canada in general, that as regards the selecting of their future citizens the interests of the Dominion and the United States are identical, and that the two governments, in justice to all concerned, must unite in announcing to those contemplating emigration from countries of the old world, that only those will be given welcome who come meeting the requirements of law, and who may be regarded as an asset to one of the two countries if permitted to land at a Canadian ocean port.

Respectfully,

JOHN H. CLARK, *Commissioner.*

Hon. F. P. SARGENT,
Commissioner-General of Immigration, Washington, D. C.

STATIONS.

During the year appreciable progress has been made in the way of securing new buildings at some of the stations where accommodations for the arriving aliens and examining officers are most needed, and in enlarging and improving such accommodations where such facilities already exist.

Thus the new station constructed at Honolulu, Hawaii, so urgently needed, has been nearly completed and will soon be in use, thereby furnishing relief from hardships to both officers and aliens and assuring a more effective administration at that port.

At New Orleans, La., and El Paso, Tex., arrangements have been made for the lease of suitable buildings for the same use, a step that has been wisely taken for the reason, shown elsewhere in this report, that both of those stations are destined to become important ports of entry for aliens, as they have long been the gateways through which Chinese of the prohibited class have secured unlawful residence in the United States.

It is especially gratifying to report that the initial steps have been taken for the erection of a commodious station building at San Francisco. This has long been needed, not alone because of the necessity for such a structure for the care of those waiting examination under the immigration laws, but because that port is the one to which most of the Chinese applicants for admission are brought. The lack of Government quarters there, and the consequent necessity of depending upon such a building as the steamship companies bringing Chinese passengers were willing to furnish, account for most of the odium which has so unjustly been charged against the enforcement of the exclusion acts. Ten acres of land on Angel Island have been transferred by the Secretary of War to the Department as a site for the projected buildings, and as soon as practicable ample accommodations will be furnished for all aliens coming to San Francisco.

The proceedings in ejectment, reported heretofore, have been settled and the title to Ellis Island cleared of all incumbrance, thus removing the only obstacle to utilizing the appropriations already made by Congress to enlarge the area of the island, for the construction of a hospital building thereon, and in other ways to increase the facilities for prompt and effective inspection of the heavy immigration to the port of New York.

It is impracticable to take up and report the work during the year at each individual station without so enlarging this report as to make it cumbrous. Suffice it to say that the pressure of work at each of them has been exceptionally exacting in character and large in amount; that the inspectors and subordinate officers and the commissioners at the larger ports have cheerfully and efficiently discharged the onerous duties imposed upon them, and that the organization of the service has proved its ability to stand any reasonable strain that is likely to be put upon it by increased immigration.

An exception, however, must be made in the case of New York, which is the receiving station for the great bulk of alien arrivals, amounting to the unprecedented monthly average during March, April, May, and June of something in excess of 100,000 persons. Commissioner Watchorn reports:

OFFICE OF COMMISSIONER OF IMMIGRATION,
New York, N. Y., July 1, 1905.

SIR:
` * * * * * * *

During the calendar year ended June 30, 1905, there were examined at this port 821,169 aliens. Of this number 98,428 were examined on board ship—they being cabin passengers. Of the number of cabin passengers thus examined, 2,982 were detained for further examination at Ellis Island. The total number of cabin passengers deported during said year was 102. During this same period 722,741 steerage passengers were examined at the port of New York. Of this number 715,663 were admitted and 7,078 were deported; so that the total number of deportations was 7,180. In addition there were also examined 126,296 passengers who presented indubitable proofs of citizenship, and, although their examination required just as much care and time as that of aliens, they do not, of course, appear in the returns of alien passengers.

During the fiscal year 1,375 aliens, who had been excluded by the "board of special inquiry" and ordered deported, appealed from such excluding decision to the Secretary of Commerce and Labor. These appeals were disposed of in the following manner: 667 were ordered landed (84 of these were admitted on bond), and 686 were ordered deported. Twenty-two appeals were pending on June 30.

Four hundred and thirty-seven alien stowaways arrived at the port of New York during the fiscal year.

* * * * * * *

To receive, examine, and dispose of 821,169 aliens in one fiscal year is a work so stupendous that none but painstaking students of the immigration service could possibly have any intelligent conception of what arduous duties and unusual considerations it involves. Large numbers of each day's arrivals are for various causes detained at Ellis Island for many days, and all of those deported are usually detained from one to two weeks, pending the next sailing of a vessel of the line bringing them. During periods of detention they must needs be fed, sheltered, furnished beds, baths, etc., and their friends must be communicated with—some 30,000 telegrams being sent to relatives and friends, as many received in reply, during the past fiscal year. In addition some 10,000 letters addressed to detained aliens were received at this office and delivered to the addressees.

No less than 16,555 remittances, aggregating $260,891.85, were received for detained aliens or persons expected to arrive, under a system so perfect as to insure prompt and accurate delivery. The payees received the amounts specified with the exception of $27,757.25, which were returned to the senders, delivery in these cases being impracticable.

* * * * * * *

No matter what the provocation, the Ellis Island officials must always be kindly disposed and mete out to each day's contingent of immigrants—to every man, woman, and child—the fullest possible measure of courteous consideration; and it is unquestionably due to their individual tact, good nature, and efficiency that so vast an army of people, unfamiliar with our tongue and unacquainted with our customs, were examined and every essential statistical fact concerning them carefully recorded and permanently kept, and every one of them treated politely; and this same spirit of kindness and sympathy was shown to those who were unfortunate enough to be adjudged inadmissible, and their deportation was effected with every degree of compassion becoming a great and powerful nation. This method of procedure has been so satisfactory that the year has passed without serious complaints being made against the policy pursued here—a fact which may be regarded as eloquent testimony to the efficiency of the Service.

* * * * * * *

That less than 1 per cent of the aliens arriving at this port were deported is a very remarkable fact and is due in no small degree, as already stated, to the various sections referred to of the act of March 3, 1903. Only 77 per 10,000 were deported, leaving 9,923 in every 10,000 to be accounted for in the numbers of those who were admitted. There can be no question but some of those who were admitted will certainly fail to be of any benefit to the communities in which they may settle; and it may well be that many of them will be added to the 44,985 alien inmates of charitable institutions in the United States reported on page 51 of the Commissioner-General's report for the year ended June 30, 1904.

* * * * * * *

Sixty-three legal actions have been brought under the different sections of the immigration law, resulting as follows:

Convictions	10
Acquittals	4
Discontinued or dismissed	10
Pending	a 39
Cases considered on Department warrant	135
Cases of deserting seamen investigated	1,351
Cases of arriving aliens not produced for examination at time of arrival	229
Writs of habeas corpus answered	30
Fraudulent citizenship cases reported to the district attorney in which convictions resulted	206
Fines resulting from said naturalization cases	$3,800

The Bureau can not fail to be favorably impressed with the good work done in connection with these fraudulent naturalization cases. All the aliens concerned, after cancellation of their naturalization certificates and the expiration of such penalties as the courts imposed on them, were subsequently treated as aliens and were either admitted or deported, as the circumstances warranted under the immigration laws.

* * * * * * *

Respectfully,

ROBERT WATCHORN, *Commissioner.*

Hon. F. P. SARGENT,
Commissioner-General of Immigration, Washington, D. C.

Commissioner Watchorn speaks in terms of high commendation of the work of the medical officers at Ellis Island, in which the Bureau unreservedly concurs, and which it extends to the officers of the United States Public Health and Marine-Hospital Service engaged in the inspection of alien arrivals at the various ports, to whose capable

---

a Indictments have been returned in 34 of the pending cases.

work the people of the United States owe much of the protection provided for by the immigration laws.

The chief medical officer at Ellis Island, Dr. George W. Stoner, makes a report of the work of his staff during the year, from which the following is taken:

ELLIS ISLAND, NEW YORK HARBOR, *July 1, 1905.*

SIR:

*   *   *   *   *   *   *

Eight hundred and twenty-one thousand one hundred and twenty-eight aliens were examined upon arrival, 98,387 were cabin passengers and 722,741 came in the steerage.

In addition to the above there were examined 93,311 cabin passengers and 33,026 steerage passengers who, upon further examination by the immigrant inspectors, proved to be citizens of the United States.

Six thousand six hundred and ninety-five aliens were certified for physical or mental defects; 793 of these were afflicted with diseases classified as dangerous, contagious, or loathsome; 95 insane, idiotic, or epileptic, and 47 were mentally weak or feeble-minded.

One thousand six hundred and twenty-nine were certified for senility, 279 for poor physique, 1,526 for hernia, 258 for valvular disease of the heart and the remainder (more than 2,000) for other diseases or physical conditions affecting ability to earn a living, as set forth in the tables accompanying and made a part of this report.

In addition to certificate cases proper 26,424 arriving aliens having minor defects were brought to the attention of the immigrant inspectors.

Six thousand three hundred and five aliens, including 185 applying for relief after landing, were admitted to hospitals for care and treatment, as follows: Immigrant hospital, Ellis Island, 4,828; Long Island College Hospital, 546; city health department hospital (acute contagious diseases), 931; total, 6,305. (See table.)

The contracts with the Long Island College Hospital and with the city health department hospital were continued during the year, and the same have been renewed for the ensuing year.

*   *   *   *   *   *

The staff of medical officers was increased during the latter part of the fiscal year; 16 medical officers were required for the three different divisions of the work—(1) on the line and in adjoining examination rooms in main building, (2) immigrant hospital, and (3) examination of cabin passengers on board incoming vessels in the bay. And in view of the enlarged facilities recently provided for the registry division by the Commissioner—the improvement and increase in the number of lines, an immigrant inspector and interpreter at the end of each line, ready to receive the immigrants as soon as they are passed along from the medical lines or turned over from the medical examination rooms—a corresponding increase in the number of medical officers detailed by the Surgeon-General will probably be required.

*   *   *   *   *   *

Respectfully,

GEO. W. STONER,
Surgeon, Public Health and Marine-Hospital Service,
Chief Medical Officer.

The COMMISSIONER OF IMMIGRATION,
Ellis Island, N. Y.

SUMMARY OF HOSPITAL TRANSACTIONS FISCAL YEAR ENDING JUNE 30, 1905.

Number of patients in hospital at beginning of year	158
Patients admitted to hospital during year	6,305
Total treated (men, 3,094; women, 1,481; male children, 959; female children, 929)	6,463
Births (male, 4; female, 6)	10
Deaths (men, 32; women, 12; male children, 68; female children, 49)	151
Pay patients treated during the year	6,308
Free patients treated during the year	155
Days treatment for pay patients	55,447
Days treatment for free patients	2,202
Total days treatment for hospital cases	57,649
Daily average number of patients in hospital	158
Patients in hospital at end of year	213

DETAILED REPORT OF HOSPITAL TRANSACTIONS.

Hospital.	Remaining from previous year.	Admitted to hospital during the year.	Total treated.	Recovered.	Improved.	Not improved.	Died.	Remaining at end of year.	Days treatment.
Immigrant hospital	71	4,828	4,899	2,704	1,027	1,027	47	94	31,066
Health department	71	931	1,002	861			79	62	18,894
Immigrant wards of the Long Island College Hospital	16	546	562	400	22	48	35	57	7,689
Total	158	6,305	6,463	3,965	1,049	1,075	161	213	57,649

APPEALS TO THE DEPARTMENT.

The accompanying table shows that during the year there have been taken an aggregate of 1,921 appeals from the decisions of boards of special inquiry at all the ports.

APPEALS FROM DECISIONS OF BOARDS, FISCAL YEAR ENDED JUNE 30, 1905.

Port.	Appeals sustained.	Appeals dismissed.	Total appeals decided.
Ellis Island	667	686	1,353
Boston	136	165	301
Philadelphia	14	20	34
Baltimore	29	53	82
San Francisco	2	2	4
Montreal	26	38	64
San Juan	3	8	11
Key West	0	1	1
New Orleans	27	37	64
Galveston	0	1	1
El Paso, Tex	0	2	2
Seattle	0	4	4
Total	904	1,017	1,921

It is impossible to examine the ultimate disposal of these appeals without being impressed by the large proportion of reversals of the boards—nearly one-half. The necessary inference as to the capacity of those who serve as members of the boards might not be so surprising if the ratio of reversals was smaller at such ports as Ellis Island and Boston, where the number of available officers for this purpose is large and where the amount of work done gives assurance that they are of unsurpassed training and soundness of judgment; but the reverse is the case. If, in nearly half of the appealed decisions rendered by the boards, after a careful inquiry, at which the aliens directly concerned and their witnesses are personally present, and thus an opportunity is afforded to pass upon the credibility of the testimony which the Department does not have when considering the appeal, those bodies are in error, and have put the aliens concerned to so much delay and expense and the Department to so much unnecessary labor, the conclusion follows inevitably that there is a radical defect in this feature of the administration which calls for amendment, both in the interest of the wrongfully detained alien and of economy of cost and labor.

The Bureau is not prepared to concede the natural inference that its boards are incompetent. On the contrary, both in natural and acquired capability, they are in their constituent elements far superior to the average petit jury, the means by which the common law determines issues of fact.   There are doubtless some improvements that could be made in the constitution of the boards, but the Bureau doubts, under existing methods of administration, whether any, the most effective, change in the personnel of the boards would materially alter the results.

The law constitutes these boards the judges.   If a board finds upon the evidence before it that an alien is likely to become a public charge, that fact should be regarded as established beyond question unless clearly against the weight of evidence.   Frequent errors of judgment as to the weight and significance of evidence is a reason for reconstituting the board guilty of such errors, and a reason that should be imperative.   But to maintain the same boards and reverse them in approximately half of the cases appealed is to maintain a practice as ineffective of its design as it is unjust to the alien whose rights are thereby affected.

The trouble is, the Bureau believes, that appeals are not treated as such, but as new trials.   Appellants should be denied such new trials, with the usual incidents of new evidence not shown to have been unattainable for presentation before the boards at the original or adjourned hearings by them, and the resort to influences which would never receive consideration by the courts under similar conditions. No new trials should be given except by the boards of special inquiry, and all appeals to the Department should be strictly treated as such and appellants required to establish, upon the record transmitted, manifest error on the part of the boards.

Any other course must lead to such conditions as those presented in the foregoing tables, and must, moreover, deprive the boards of the benefit of an assurance that their decisions are respected and that it is worth while, whatever they may think of the merits of a case, to follow a decision rendered by them upon substantially the same evidence as that presented by a case in which they have been reversed.

In other words, the remedy lies in good boards, governed by appropriate regulations, a hearing and an appeal therefrom instead of a new trial, without specifically assigned error, upon written testimony after an original one upon oral testimony.

NEW IMMIGRATION LEGISLATION.

An additional year of experience has confirmed the views expressed a year ago in regard to the necessity for new or amendatory legislation to regulate the immigration of aliens into the United States.   In another part of the report the subject of diseased aliens has been treated at some length, and the facts stated therein sustain the recommendation made for several years past, and now reiterated, that suitable steps be taken to locate competent medical officers at the principal foreign ports of embarkation, to require that all aliens seeking passage to this country secure as a prerequisite a certificate of good health, mental and physical, from one of such officers, and that the bringing of any alien unprovided with such a certificate to a port of this country shall subject the vessel by which he is so brought to summary fine. If, for any reason, such a course as that set forth is impracticable, it is urged that the penalty of $100 now prescribed in section 9 of the immigration law of March 3, 1903, be increased to $500.

In the last annual report the terms of a circular were given which showed the means to which one of the great transportation lines resorted to avoid on the one hand the loss of business entailed by refusal to carry aliens afflicted with communicable diseases, and on the other hand to shift to the shoulders of the diseased immigrant the penalty for its own misdeeds. The increased penalty will not only operate to prevent such a recourse by companies which only regard the law so far as requisite to escape its punishment, but will also necessitate the exercise of greater care by those lines which have a respect for the law but find an occasional payment of $100 less onerous than the constant provision of competent medical inspection.

The Bureau recommends, besides, such further legislation as will enable the Government to punish those who induce aliens to come to this country under promise or assurance of employment. As elsewhere stated, it is useless to anticipate any effective exclusion of such aliens until it is made possible to inflict such penalties on the employers who violate the law as will deter the latter from taking such risks. The defect in the existing laws seems not to be in the insufficiency of the penalty, but rather in the difficulty, under the laws of evidence which apply in penal actions, of proving the responsibility for the offense committed. Such legislation, therefore, to be effective should establish rules of evidence less exacting, as well as provide for some summary mode of trial.

Again, it is urged that Congress provide means for distributing arriving aliens who now congregate in the large cities. The reasons for this recommendation have already been fully stated in former reports as well as in the appropriate place in this, and do not require repetition here.

As a means of preventing a further increase of alien immigration it will be necessary, if such a policy is deemed expedient, either to enlarge the prohibited classes by adding thereto those who are illiterate; those whom age or feebleness renders incapable of self-support, if at all, but temporarily and under the most favorable conditions; those who have not brought a sufficient sum of money to enable them to maintain themselves for a reasonable time in the event of sickness or temporary lack of employment; or else to adopt adequate means, enforced by sufficient penalties, to compel steamship companies engaged in the passenger business to observe in good faith the law which forbids them to encourage or solicit immigration to the United States. If all other means are found ineffective it might be not unwise to borrow a device of the Canadian laws which has long been used as an effective check on Chinese immigration—a limitation upon vessels coming to its ports, apportioning the number of such passengers in a direct ratio to the tonnage of such vessels. The only reasonable objection to such a measure would be, not to its nature, but to the ratio adopted. Its merit lies in the fact that by it the constitutionality of the power of Congress to regulate commerce could thus be made effective for the first time as regards the bringing of aliens in unlimited numbers to this country. The ratio, of course, would depend upon the views of Congress as to the degree of restriction during any period which should be imposed on alien immigration.

New legislation is recommended to make the decisions of boards of special inquiry of more effect, specifically by requiring that all evidence not presented before such boards be excluded from consideration on appeal, as well as that new trials should not be granted either by the boards or by the Department for the consideration of new evidence unless it clearly appears that such evidence was unattainable at the original hearing. Provision should also be made that the decisions of the boards, or of the Department on appeal, shall be final only when adverse to the admission of an alien.

It is further recommended, as has also been done in former reports, that the provision of law which, for the first time in 1903, after twenty-one years' continuous practice to the contrary, abolished the head tax on account of alien passengers intending to land at our ports for transit through the United States to some foreign country, be repealed. All the embarrassments which it was feared would result from that change have been experienced, and the relief to the companies responsible for the payment of the tax has been trivial. Moreover, if such tax, as doubtless is the case, has been included in the transportation charges, it is not the carrier who is entitled to relief, but the transit passenger. It is safe to say that none of such passengers ever secures the smallest benefit from the exemption, except possibly those entering through foreign contiguous territory.

To obviate difficulties of administration it is recommended that any alien who has been domiciled in Canada or Mexico for more than one year be exempt from the payment of the head tax, as are citizens of those countries under section 1 of the immigration act of March 3, 1903.

Legislation should be adopted to check violations of the immigration laws by professed seamen, thus taking advantage of their status acquired under one law to escape the operation of another. Such legislation should impose a sufficient penalty upon masters of vessels for signing other than bona fide seamen upon their crew lists, thus enabling such pretended seamen to enter this country without the examination made of all other aliens by simply deserting after arrival at our ports. Masters of vessels should be required to notify inspection officers upon arrival and before departure from ports of this country, so that such officers may be able to ascertain whether aliens brought thereon have departed, if inadmissible to the United States. The masters should also be held accountable for any alien seaman brought by them who, he is informed by an immigrant inspector, should be retained on board as an inadmissible alien, as they are for the escape of alien passengers denied a landing.

The Bureau also repeats, for the reasons then stated, its recommendation of one year ago, that, as a means of ascertaining the net annual increase of our alien population, masters of vessels be required as a precedent to obtaining clearance papers from ports of this country to furnish to the immigration officers lists or manifests of outgoing alien passengers on such vessels, prepared and verified in like manner as the manifests or lists of arriving aliens.

SPECIAL RECOMMENDATIONS.

In addition to the new legislation above urged, there are two other measures that have long seemed to me to offer the means of controlling immigration to this country, so as to prevent the hardships which inevitably arise from the refusal of permission to land at our ports to those aliens who are excluded by section 2 of the law.

Of these, the first is intended to enlighten aliens as to the provisions of our laws, so that they may not in ignorance sever their home ties and sacrifice their small possessions in an ineffectual attempt to enter the United States. For this purpose it is suggested that suitable steps be taken, by special legislation for the purpose, if that be necessary, to have the laws and regulations translated into the various tongues represented by our alien immigration, and that such translations be distributed widely in foreign countries, either through the agency of the Department of State or in such other way as will accomplish the purpose of generally furnishing intending immigrants with the means of acting understandingly as to their admissibility to this country. It is, of course, impossible to say how many will be influenced by such a knowledge, in view of the promises made to them by the agents of transportation lines, but it will at least accomplish the purpose of Congress in requiring, fruitlessly, it is believed, the said lines to post such translations at their foreign ticket agencies, and will relieve this country of any responsibility, through inaction, for the needless distress and suffering of rejected aliens coming to our ports under the delusion that they may be allowed to land.

The second measure is designed to secure, by treaty or convention, the cooperation of foreign countries from which aliens migrate hither, both in reducing the number of immigrants and preventing the inadmissible and undesirable classes from leaving their own homes. With this end in view, it is urged that an international conference be arranged for, to be held at some suitable or accessible place either in the United States or abroad, and to be constituted of delegates or conferees from each country participating therein. These delegates should be men of practical experience in handling immigrants and of broad intelligence in their views on the subject. Such a conference would, it is believed, be conducive to a good understanding between the various nationalities taking part therein, would enlighten each as to the purposes and wishes of the others in regard to this most important subject, would doubtless secure, as to points agreed upon, an effective restraint of the transportation agencies, and finally would throw such a light upon the attitude of foreign governments towards our present system of immigration restriction as would enable Congress to decide intelligently what additional measures are necessary to protect this country from the dangers of an increasing influx of aliens.

Such conferences have been held on postal laws and other utilitarian subjects, but none of them, in my judgment, is comparable, in its direct bearing upon the welfare of our people and country, to that presented by our growing alien population. The benefits that have resulted from those conferences furnish reasonable assurance that the same resort will not be without useful results in the effective control of immigration.

EXCLUSION OF CHINESE.

In no branch of its widespread activities does the Bureau believe that it has so thoroughly succeeded in carrying into effective operation the purpose of the laws committed to its charge as in the exclusion of Chinese of the classes which it is the professed desire of both this Government and the Empire of China to keep out of the United States. As pointed out in former reports, there are many and serious obstacles, both in the circumstances to be dealt with by administrative officers and in the opposition of many citizens of this country to the policy of selecting the Chinese alone as subjects for exclusion, that exact of the Bureau a degree of vigilance and resourcefulness unexampled, it is believed, in the administration of any other legislation on the statute books. Representatives of the large missionary interests do not hesitate to express openly their disapproval of the law or to denounce those whose duty it is to administer the law. The commercial interests of the country, while more prudent and self-restrained in their utterances on the subject, are equally opposed both to the policy and to the means necessarily used to make that policy effective. A large and somewhat vociferous element sympathize with the foregoing classes. This element is composed in part of those who can not see any greater risk at stake than the probable reduction of the price of labor in this country, of those who are persuaded that Chinese would engage in agricultural labor in the Southern States and constitute a more reliable system than that now available there, and of those who hold the illogical opinion that because alleged undesirable aliens of other races are being allowed to enter the United States this country is compelled by some fancied rule of consistency or propriety to admit other undesirable aliens of the Chinese race.

Of course it is not questioned that all of these persons are entitled to entertain such views, or any views, but the only proper means of giving them expression in law is by a resort to Congress. The course pursued, however, is denunciation of the officers who enforce the law and misrepresentation of their acts, made either in willful disregard of the truth or in ignorance, and published abroad either through the public press or by any other means which promises to secure such frequent repetition as may serve to invest falsehood with a semblance of truth. Occasionally such opposition finds expression in language, if not overt acts of resistance to the officers, and instances are not lacking of judicial officers justifying the release of Chinese found unlawfully in the United States, on the ground that they have never approved the law; one such officer going so far as to denounce it as "a relic of medieval barbarism," and one judge suspending sentence of deportation indefinitely in the case of a Chinese defendant who could not be discharged upon the evidence even by one who was opposed to exclusion. Such instances of judicial resistance are rare, fortunately, but they serve to show the attitude of opposition which conflicts with the discharge of their duty by Chinese inspectors.

That it has recently become so pronounced affords the Bureau, and should the public, likewise, the most convincing evidence that the present administration is effective, despite the extent and persistency of the resistance above described.

There is, however, a far more serious obstacle than any above recited. It is all the more serious because it can not be located precisely, nor can the individuals or organizations through whose exertions it is raised be identified. There is no Chinese steerage passenger so destitute that money practically without limit is not available to pay for his entrance. He can command legal advice of the most expensive counselors; he can secure witnesses to testify to anything; he can tempt smugglers by payment of large sums of money; he can carry his case through all the tribunals up to the Supreme Court of the United States. His youth, his obvious ignorance, his equally conspicuous poverty, his lack of friends or relatives known to him in this country, his lack of knowledge even of the occupation to which he will apply himself if landed—all combined do not deprive him of the benefit of ample funds from some source to secure his admission in some way, if possible. It is not unsafe to say that more money has been expended by the few Chinese immigrants during the past year, aggregating a little less than 2,000, than by the million or more other aliens, in the attempt to secure admission after arrival at our ports.

This large expenditure, taken in connection with the cost of transportation and the expense of subsistence while awaiting a final decision as to the right of Chinese aliens to land, leads to the irresistible conclusion that Chinese immigration is systematically exploited by some organization which must find its returns in the well-known faithfulness of the race in the payment of its debts. This view is confirmed by many circumstances, among which may be reckoned the reported recent contributions of the members of the merchant class in this country to the agitation of the boycott in China against American goods, which has for its purpose the repeal of the exclusion laws, and the dissemination of such misstatements as are calculated to mislead those in this country who are ignorant of the methods of administering the law. Although, as stated, the precise source of this potent influence can not be established with certainty, it is·felt every day by administrative officers through its obstructive operation.

Those who openly denounce exclusion as now enforced assume an attitude of fairness by asserting that they favor a strict application of the law to "laborers," who only are included, they aver, in the intent of the law and treaties. In a sense this is true, although the laws on this subject for ten years or more past are avowedly to exclude "Chinese persons and persons of Chinese descent." It is misleading, however, since it produces upon the public mind the idea that the word "laborer" is used in the treaty and laws in the popular sense. For twenty-five years it has been construed by judicial and executive authority to represent all Chinese persons who were not specifically enumerated in the treaty of 1880 as entitled to come to this country, and thus to have a wholly different meaning as regards the right of entry into and residence within the United States from its popular interpretation.· The judicial and executive rulings upon this point, which have been repeatedly denounced as arbitrary and unauthorized, are supported by the best possible authority, to wit, the negotiators, on behalf of both of the contracting Governments, of the treaty of 1880, on which all of the existing exclusion laws are based. These gentlemen, who must have known the purport of the language they used, are on record as according with the interpretations denounced as unauthorized.

If it has been difficult in the past to exclude laborers posing as members of one of the four exempt classes, how greatly such difficulties would be multiplied if the classes of which they might successfully pretend to be members were extended to traders, doctors, lawyers, farmers, engineers, priests, clerks, and the countless avocations bordering on manual labor. Such an interpretation the Bureau believes would make the law as inoperative to exclude laborers as would be an "open door" to all Chinese. To favor the exclusion of Chinese laborers therefore does not consist with the advocacy of the view criticized any more than it does with an endeavor to relax those rules and regulations which have grown up in the course of administration as a result of the deceit and resourcefulness of violators of the law.

The Bureau has no hesitation in denying, without mental reservation or qualification, the oft-repeated charges that, through its officers, Chinese persons seeking admission to this country, whether of high or low degree measured by the caste laws of their own country, have been subjected to insult or humiliation or indignity. If such had been the case, the way has always been open to remedy the fault or prevent its recurrence by establishing the truth of any specific charge of official misconduct. There is no special immunity enjoyed by officers of this Bureau, as distinguished from other branches of the Executive Government, from the consequences of their actions. The truth is that such complaints can be made only in a general and indefinite way to gain currency; specific instances would, as they have been in the very few instances when given, promptly be shown to be without foundation. Thus a charge only specific so far as to allege ill treatment of the student class at San Francisco and the consequent resentment of that class and resort to other countries for education, was promptly met by incontrovertible proof that every member, except two, of that class applying at the said port since the formation of this Department, had been promptly admitted, most of them directly from the steamship, the two exceptions being denied under the immigration law because they had trachoma, a dangerous contagious disease.

In concluding these prefatory remarks, the Bureau expresses the firm conviction that, whatever the original source of the present agitation against the enforcement of the exclusion laws may be, the purpose in view will not be content with any modification of present modes of administration, however extensive. An influence sufficiently potent, by using the boycott against a great nation, to secure the relaxation of regulations which have been enforced for years, which are believed to be just and necessary, and which have successfully passed ordeals before the judicial branch of the Government, will have secured assurance that it may likewise influence the legislation of the nation, and will be emboldened to demand all it wants—the emasculation, if not repeal, of the exclusion policy.

APPLICATIONS FOR ADMISSION.

The following tables give the number of applications by Chinese persons during the year for admission to the United States, the grounds of such applications, the action taken thereon, and whether such action was taken by the inspectors, the Department, or the courts:

TABLE 1.—CHINESE SEEKING ADMISSION TO THE UNITED STATES DURING THE FISCAL YEAR ENDED JUNE 30, 1905.

BORDER CASES.

	Total cases.	New applications.	Pending from previous year.	Finally admitted.	Deported.	Pending close current year.
United States citizens	30	30	....	26	3	1
Returning laborers	59	52	7	42	11	6
Returning merchants	127	114	13	99	22	6
Other merchants	44	44	....	34	10	....
Merchants' wives	10	10	....	8	2	....
Merchants' children	19	19	....	15	2	2
Other exempt classes	45	44	1	42	3	....
Total	334	313	21	266	53	15

TABLE 1.—CHINESE SEEKING ADMISSION TO THE UNITED STATES DURING THE FISCAL YEAR ENDED JUNE 30, 1905—Continued.

SEAPORT CASES.

	Total cases.	New applications.	Pending from previous year.	Finally admitted.	Deported.	Pending close current year.
United States citizens	752	578	174	608	67	77
Returning laborers	637	572	65	581	46	10
Returning merchants	517	460	57	449	48	20
Other merchants	441	305	136	245	194	2
Merchants' wives	31	27	4	28	3	....
Merchants' children	140	110	30	108	20	12
Other exempt classes	370	362	8	320	50	....
Total	2,888	2,414	474	2,339	428	121

TOTAL.

	Total cases.	New applications.	Pending from previous year.	Finally admitted.	Deported.	Pending close current year.
United States citizens	782	608	174	634	70	78
Returning laborers	696	624	72	623	57	16
Returning merchants	644	574	70	548	70	26
Other merchants	485	349	136	279	204	2
Merchants' wives	41	37	4	36	5	....
Merchants' children	159	129	30	123	22	14
Other exempt classes	415	406	9	362	53	....
Total	3,222	2,727	495	2,605	451	136
In transit	741	741	....	739	2	....

BY PORTS.

	Total cases.	New applications.	Pending from previous year.	Finally admitted.	Deported.	Pending close current year.
San Francisco, Cal	2,315	1,880	435	1,838	364	113
Portland, Oreg	8	8	....	5	3	....
Port Townsend, Wash	306	276	30	244	54	8
Honolulu, Hawaii	249	240	9	243	6	....
Sumas, Wash	157	157	....	127	20	10
Portal, N. Dak	57	49	8	46	11	....
Malone, N. Y	91	80	11	67	19	5
Richford, Vt	29	27	2	26	3	....
New York, N. Y	9	9	....	8	1	....
New Orleans, La	1	1	....	1	....	....
Total	3,222	2,727	495	2,605	481	136

TABLE 2.—CHINESE SEEKING ADMISSION TO THE UNITED STATES DURING THE FISCAL YEAR ENDED JUNE 30, 1905.

BORDER CASES.

	Admissions.			Rejections.			Cases pending.			Cases finally disposed of.	
	By inspectors.	By Department.	By courts.	By inspectors.	By Department.	By courts.	Before inspectors.	Before Department.	Before courts.	Admitted.	Deported.
United States citizens	24	2	....	5	1	....	1	....	....	26	3
Returning laborers	42	....	....	12	4	....	6	....	....	42	11
Returning merchants	95	4	....	24	5	....	6	....	....	99	22
Other merchants	34	....	....	8	5	....	....	....	....	54	10
Merchants' wives	8	....	....	2	....	....	....	....	....	8	2
Merchants' children	14	1	....	4	....	....	....	....	2	15	2
Other exempt classes	41	....	1	2	1	....	....	....	....	42	3
Total	258	7	1	57	16	....	13	....	2	266	53

TABLE 2.—CHINESE SEEKING ADMISSION TO THE UNITED STATES DURING THE FISCAL YEAR ENDED JUNE 30, 1905—Continued.

SEAPORT CASES.

	Admissions.			Rejections.			Cases pending.			Cases finally disposed of.	
	By inspectors.	By Department.	By courts.	By inspectors.	By Department.	By courts.	Before inspectors.	Before Department.	Before courts.	Admitted.	Deported.
'United States citizens	515	29	81	96	136	35	50	......	27	608	67
Returning laborers	557	24	....	57	16	....	10	......	....	581	46
Returning merchants	438	11	....	56	8	....	19	1	....	449	48
Other merchants	215	30	....	220	140	....	2	......	....	246	194
Merchants' wives	26	2	....	4	....	....	......	......	....	28	3
Merchants' children	98	10	....	20	9	....	12	......	....	108	20
Other exempt classes	320	....	....	49	....	....	......	......	....	320	50
Total	2,169	106	81	502	309	35	98	1	27	2,339	428

TOTAL.

	By inspectors.	By Department.	By courts.	By inspectors.	By Department.	By courts.	Before inspectors.	Before Department.	Before courts.	Admitted.	Deported.
United States citizens	539	31	81	101	137	35	51	......	27	634	70
Returning laborers	599	24	....	69	20	....	16	......	....	623	57
Returning merchants	533	15	....	80	13	....	25	1	....	548	70
Other merchants	249	30	....	228	145	....	2	......	....	279	204
Merchants' wives	34	2	....	6	....	....	......	......	....	36	5
Merchants' children	112	11	....	24	9	....	12	......	2	123	22
Other exempt classes	361	......	1	51	1	....	......	......	....	362	53
Total	2,427	113	82	559	325	35	106	1	29	2,605	481
In transit	739	......	....	2	......	....	......	......	....	739	2

BY PORTS.

	By inspectors.	By Department.	By courts.	By inspectors.	By Department.	By courts.	Before inspectors.	Before Department.	Before courts.	Admitted.	Deported.
San Francisco, Cal	1,677	97	81	429	300	35	86	......	27	1,838	364
Portland, Oreg	5	....	....	3	....	....	......	......	....	5	3
Port Townsend, Wash	237	7	....	59	7	....	7	1	....	244	54
Honolulu, Hawaii	241	2	....	10	2	....	......	......	....	243	6
Sumas, Wash	124	3	....	23	8	....	10	......	....	127	20
Portal, N. Dak	46	....	....	12	2	....	......	......	....	46	11
Malone, N. Y	62	4	1	16	6	....	3	......	2	67	19
Richford, Vt	26	....	....	6	....	....	......	......	....	26	3
New York, N. Y	8	....	....	1	....	....	......	......	....	8	1
New Orleans, La	1	....	....	....	....	....	......	......	....	1	......
Total	2,427	113	82	569	325	35	106	1	29	2,605	481

SUMMARY.

Classes.	Admitted.	Deported.
United States citizens	631	70
Returning laborers	623	57
Returning merchants	548	70
Other merchants	279	204
Members of merchants' families	159	27
Other exempt classes	362	53
Total	2,605	481

Of the 2,605 admitted, 1,805 were residents returning to the United States and 800 were new arrivals Of the 481 deported, 197 claimed to be residents and 284 new arrivals.

Of the total admissions and deportations there were admitted at San Francisco 1,838, and deported from that port 364 during the year.

As bearing upon the alleged severity of the officers at the ports it is noteworthy that of 741 who applied for the privilege of passing through the United States to foreign countries but 2 were denied, although the Bureau has long believed, upon strong corroborative evidence, that in most instances, practically in all where the transit sought is to the Republic of Mexico, the ulterior design is merely to effect an entry into the United States over the land boundary, which presents fewer natural obstacles than the coasts.

As will be seen elsewhere, the international boundary line between this country and Mexico is now comparatively well guarded by competent officers, for which reason more liberality is exercised in granting the privilege of transit.

It should here be stated in explanation of the apparent discrepancy between the number of Chinese arrivals for the year, as shown by the tabulated statement of alien immigrants by race and as given in the table of Chinese arrivals, that the former reports Chinese aliens only, while the latter includes also persons of that race who are found on examination to be citizens of this country.

THE EXEMPT CLASSES.

Those Chinese persons, other than registered laborers, entitled to enter and reside in the United States are of two general classes—first, such as are expressly enumerated in the treaty, and, second, those whom the courts have held to be included with them, as dependents upon members of the first class, by reasonable implication. The former consists of merchants, teachers, students, and travelers; the latter of the wives and minor children of merchants.

· The merchants, moreover, are distinguished, according to domicile, into merchants of China, who alone are required to present "section 6" certificates from their home Government, and resident Chinese merchants of the United States, whose admission after temporary absence is not made upon a "section 6" certificate, but upon evidence of their individual occupation in this country as merchants during the year prior to departure.

Table 1 shows that of 618 Chinese persons claiming the right to enter the United States during the past year as domiciled merchants there were admitted, upon evidence produced solely in this country, 548, and denied, 70, the rejections amounting to about 11 per cent of the applications.

In striking contrast with this proportion is the ratio of exclusions of alleged Chinese merchants of China, whose admission in each case is dependent upon a certificate issued by their Government, both to establish their alleged mercantile status and to show the permission of such Government to the migration of the holder. Of this class, as shown by the summary following Table 1, there were 483 applicants for admission during the year, of which number 279 were admitted and 204, or 42 per cent, as compared with 11 per cent of denied returning merchants, were rejected.

What is the significance of such a discrepancy? Have the officers at the ports, and the Department on appeal from such officers, disregarded, as has been charged, the prima facie right to admission which the law says the possession of such certificates, duly viséed by a consular or diplomatic representative of this country located in China, shall give

DISPOSITION OF

CHINESE ARRIVED AT UNITED STATES PORTS

AND

CHINESE ARRESTED WITHIN THE UNITED STATES

BECAUSE HERE IN VIOLATION OF LAW

ARRIVALS	ARRESTS
EXEMPT CLASSES ADMITTED TO U. S.	CONVICTED & DEPORTED TO CHINA
RETURNING LABORERS ADMITTED TO U. S.	
ALLOWED TO PASS IN TRANSIT THROUGH U. S.	ACQUITTED & ALLOWED TO REMAIN IN U. S.
DENIED ADMISSION TO U. S.	

the holders thereof? The mere statement of the question, coupled with the pregnant fact that the remaining 58 per cent of such applicants were allowed to enter, should be a sufficient negative reply. The Administration can have no possible interest to exclude Chinese except its obligation to enforce the law; if the complaint was because of the number admitted, then, to those who are prone to regard all officials as dishonest, there might be cause of suspicion of improper conduct, for it is notorious that the Chinese have control of money and are willing to pay for admission, but not even the most virulent objector to the law and its agents has ever charged that funds were available, other than those appropriated by Congress, for the exclusion of Chinese.

The truth is that the officers believed that the law, which with great care enumerated the indispensable elements of a good certificate and declared that one completely conforming to such requirements constituted prima facie evidence of the holder's right to land, also imposed upon them the duty of such an inquiry as would prevent one who had obtained such evidence by fraud from benefiting by such fraud, for it also provided "but said certificates may be controverted and the facts therein stated disproved by the United States authorities." This the administrative officers did in 42 per cent of the cases of merchants of China applying last year, and by this means 204 laborers, the class which all profess a desire to shut out, were excluded.

If fault there be for this condition, it is not to seek on this side of the Pacific. Where the false evidence was prepared and approved lies the fault. More will be said further on in regard to this subject.

It is the alleged ill treatment of this class and of the students which has caused such resistance to the administration and to the laws, and which has been used to justify the resort to compulsory measures by the people of one country against those of another with which it is on terms of amity. As already shown, but two students have been excluded at San Francisco in two years, and both of those on account of disease, while 42 per cent of the alleged merchants have been supplied with false evidence by officials of their own Government.

The summary also shows that of 415 applicants of the other exempt classes 362, or 87 per cent, were admitted and 53 were excluded.

During the year 186 applied for admission, under the court decisions referred to, as the wives and minor children of merchants, of whom 159, or 80 per cent, were allowed to land and 27 were rejected.

More will be said, in treating the subject of new legislation, of registered laborers. Here it will be sufficient to call attention to the figures, which show that of the 680 Chinese persons who sought admission as returning laborers there were 623 admitted during the year and 57 refused.

ARRIVALS AND DEPARTURES OF REGISTERED CHINESE LABORERS DURING FISCAL YEAR ENDED JUNE 30, 1905.

Port.	Departure of laborers.	Return of laborers.	Port.	Departure of laborers.	Return of laborers.
San Francisco, Cal	275	304	Richford, Vt	14	16
Port Townsend, Wash....	31	99	Portal, N. Dak	11	6
Portland, Oreg	....	1	Sumas, Wash	26	9
Honolulu, Hawaii........	130	177			
Malone, N. Y.............	13	11	Total...............	500	623

ALLEGED NATIVES.

Table 1 shows that during the year 608 Chinese persons sought admission to the country as citizens by birth, which, added to the unfinished cases from last year, made a total of 782 of this class. The number of new applications of such persons is exceeded only by that of returning laborers, 624.

As throwing light upon the allegations that a denial of justice results from the hearings before inspectors, chiefly because of the regulations under which such hearings are conducted, it is interesting to note that of the 640 native cases passed on by said officers 539, or 84 per cent, were admitted and but 101, or 16 per cent, excluded. The Department released, of the 168 cases of this nature appealed to it, 31, or 18 per cent, and excluded 137, or 82 per cent; while the courts, on habeas corpus, chiefly prior to departmental action on appeal, discharged, of a total of 116 finally determined, 81, or about 70 per cent. To understand the reason for such a number of reversals of the officers by the courts, it is necessary to state that by a resort to the writ of habeas corpus attorneys secured copies of the record of testimony in every case, which was forbidden by the departmental regulations, and were thus enabled to know the kind and amount of corroborative Chinese testimony needed to make cases for their clients, and when the hearing was held by a commissioner, as referee of the court issuing the writ, were permitted to introduce such new testimony, making out by this means an entirely new case.

There is no limitation in the regulations on the number of witnesses that may be introduced, although the attempt has been made to so pervert the plain language of the regulation which forbids officers to take the testimony of one witness in the presence of other witnesses in a case as to prove the contrary. The actual difficulty is to get witnesses to testify consistently with each other, a difficulty which can only be overcome by introducing one or two, suing out a writ of habeas corpus, and thus securing copies of the testimony of such witnesses. This was done so successfully that 70 per cent of the cases thus handled last year were won—solely as a result of evading a departmental regulation. Is it occasion for wonder that, since the Supreme Court, by the decision in the Ju Toy case, decided in May, has confined the hearings in habeas corpus proceedings to the record made before inspection officers, the next point of attack should be the regulations? If counsel can effect the repeal or modification of the regulations so as to secure copies of the testimony as the hearings proceed before the administrative officers, they will care nothing for the Ju Toy decision, and will suddenly become as earnest advocates for determination by such officers of claims to birth in the United States as they have heretofore been that the courts alone could rightfully pass upon facts involving a claimant's citizenship under the fourteenth amendment to the Constitution.

The Bureau therefore desires to express its unqualified disapproval of changes in existing regulations, not because it is opposed to extending every facility to Chinese persons, native born or alien, who are entitled to enter the United States to prove such right, but because it is convinced that such change will afford a means of entry for those not entitled by law or treaty to come to or reside in this country.

Attention is directed to the figures in Table 2, which show that in but two cases, other than claimants of citizenship, has there been a resort during the year from the officers to the courts. A reason for this, additional to the one already assigned, may well be that the decision of the courts, when favorable to the petitioners in such cases, clothes the claimants with all the rights of citizenship.

One of the singular and unanticipated results of the increase of Chinese citizens of this country was shown by several appeals by the wives of such citizens against the excluding decisions of the officer in charge at San Francisco. The appellants were married at a consulate of the United States in China by a Methodist missionary to young Chinamen whom the courts had determined to be citizens by birth in this country. It was in evidence that the wives had never seen their husbands until brought to the consulate to be married to them and that the purpose of such marriage was to bring appellants to this country to enter houses of ill-fame.

As these women were American citizens by virtue of their marriage, and as there is no law, and can constitutionally be no law, to banish citizens of this country for such an offense, they were admitted to pursue their intended shameless avocation should their husbands so require.

CERTIFICATES OF RESIDENCE.

The time within which Chinese persons lawfully resident in the United States could register as such and procure certificates to establish their right to be here expired May 4, 1894. The law required the arrest and deportation of Chinese laborers found in this country after that date without such certificate, but provided that if it appeared to the judicial officer before whom such arrested laborer is brought for sentence of expulsion, by the testimony of at least one credible witness other than Chinese, that he was lawfully in the United States at the time of registration and was prevented by sickness or other unavoidable cause from procuring a certificate during such time, one should be furnished him without cost. This is the only case in which an original certificate can now be issued to a Chinese laborer.

The law also provides that proof before such judicial officer that the Chinese person on trial had a certificate which had been lost or destroyed should entitle the defendant to a duplicate.

This is the sole statutory provision for the issuance of a duplicate certificate.

The executive officers, however, have for years been issuing duplicates of alleged lost certificates upon proof satisfactory to them of the loss or destruction of the original, a practice that at one time was somewhat carelessly pursued.

Since the records have been deposited with the Bureau and placed in charge of one officer the practice has been continued, though more care is now exercised to prevent frauds by Chinese who are without their original certificates because of their own fault, as is the case of those who have pledged them as security for money loaned, or who have forfeited them by leaving the United States without conforming to the requirements of law as to proof of their right to return after departure from this country.

For reasons stated in making recommendations for new legislation, the Bureau has been liberal in accepting as sufficient the proof offered to sustain such applications.

The following table shows the number of applications for duplicate certificates and the disposition thereof during the past year:

APPLICATIONS FOR CERTIFICATES OF RESIDENCE DURING THE YEAR ENDED JUNE 30, 1905.

Cases pending from previous year	99
Cases reopened	17
Applications	398
	—— 514
Duplicate certificates of residence issued	246
Original certificates of residence issued	3
Original certificates of residence found	6
New photographs affixed to certificates	1
Applications denied	83
Cases dropped	62
Cases pending	113
	—— 514

In considering the arrests, shown hereafter, the figures above should be given due weight as indicative of the desire of the Bureau to give every Chinese person lawfully in this country ample opportunity to establish such right. Should the investigations incident to such applications show in any case that the applicant had never possessed a certificate, or that he had by his own act forfeited the one issued to him, the officer in charge of the district where such applicant resides has no recourse but to arrest him as required by law.

ARREST OF UNLAWFUL CHINESE RESIDENTS.

The following table is compiled from statements furnished by United States marshals, and shows the total of arrests for the year, the courts before which the prisoners were tried, and the final disposal of the prisoners. Of the number arrested during the year, 1,110, and those pending at the close of the previous year, 292, aggregating 1,402, it is shown that 12 died or escaped, 302 were still not disposed of by the courts, 441 were discharged, and 647 were deported—thus that many more than half of those whose cases were concluded were found to be in this country in violation of law. A number of those who were liberated by the courts, moreover, owed their escape from deportation to the judicial bias already commented on, while others were, by means of that final resource of Chinese laborers, the claim of citizenship supported by Chinese testimony, enabled not only to secure a residence in this country but as well, to use the language of the Supreme Court, "the inestimable heritage of American citizenship."

The natural resort in cases of such a flagrant miscarriage of justice would be by appeal to a higher court. This right, however, is confined exclusively to the Chinese defendant in cases tried before the United States commissioners, the laws having made no provision in such cases for the exercise by the Government of the corresponding means of protecting itself from error. With this explanation it will be possible to comprehend the full significance of the statement that of the total discharges 347 were made by United States commissioners and but 94 by the courts.

ACTION TAKEN IN THE CASES OF CHINESE PERSONS ARRESTED ON THE CHARGE OF BEING IN THE UNITED STATES IN VIOLATION OF LAW, FOR FISCAL YEAR ENDED JUNE 30, 1905.

CASES BEFORE UNITED STATES COMMISSIONERS.

Arrests made during this year	1,109
Pending before hearing at close of previous year	92
Total	1,201
Bailed on personal recognizance	2
Bailed on bond	390
Total bailed before hearing	392

Disposition:

Died	3
Escaped	1
Forfeited bail	3
Discharged	347
Pending before hearing at close of present year	77
Ordered deported	770
Ordered deported this year	770
Awaiting deportation or appeal at close of previous year	50
Total	820

Disposition:

Escaped	1
Deported	549
Awaiting deportation or appeal to United States district courts at close of present year	81
Appealed to United States district courts	189

CASES BEFORE UNITED STATES DISTRICT COURTS.

Arrests (original arraignment in district court)	1
Appealed to United States district courts this year (including 11 remanded, by higher U. S. Courts)	200
Pending before trial at close of previous year	99
Total	300
Bailed on appeal to United States district courts	56

Disposition:

Forfeited bail	1
Discharged	94
Pending before trial at close of present year	108
Ordered deported	97
Ordered deported this year	97
Awaiting deportation or appeal to higher courts at close of previous year	22
Total	119

Disposition:

Died	1
Escaped	1
Deported	76
Awaiting deportation or appeal at close of present year	23
Appealed to higher courts	18

CASES BEFORE HIGHER UNITED STATES COURTS.

Appealed to higher United States courts this year	18
Pending before trial at close of previous year	29
Total	47

Disposition:
Remanded 11
Pending before trial at close of present year 13
Ordered deported 23

Ordered deported this year 23
Disposition:
Escaped 1
Deported 22

RECAPITULATION OF ALL CASES.

Arrests made this year 1,110
Pending at close of previous year, including those awaiting deportation or
appeal 292

Total 1,402
Disposition:
Died, escaped, and forfeited bail 12
Discharged 441
Deported 647
Pending at close of present year, including those awaiting deportation or
appeal 302

Before concluding this subject it may properly be said that the arrests made during the year were not the result of organized effort to discover unlawful residents. Such efforts were not made further than to locate the Chinese in the United States, whether lawfully or otherwise, primarily to facilitate the investigations incident to the claims of domiciled merchants and returning laborers seeking admission after temporary absence. The arrests were therefore chiefly incident to the discharge of other duties, such as investigations of the above-mentioned character.

The effort to locate the Chinese, which must have resulted in protection to those who were thereby ascertained to have a right to reside here, raised a storm of protest which could only be explained upon the ground that it would also expose those living here in violation of law to arrest and deportation. Such a protest, coming doubtless from the same source already referred to as unidentifiable, and backed by such a potent argument as the boycott, could not effect less than a discontinuance of further attempts in this line, which would result in discovery of violators of the laws of this country.

Before the discontinuance, however, the inspectors had located in this country many hundreds of laborers who were without the certificates of residence required by law, and who should, therefore, in the language of the acts of May 5, 1892, and November 3, 1893, "be decreed and adjudged to be unlawfully in the United States."

RULE 44.

This rule, which embodies the conditions under which Chinese persons inadmissible under the treaty and laws may be allowed to enter the United States to take part in any exposition aided by the Government, was adopted under authority of section 2 of the act of April 29, 1902. It was given in full in the last annual report, in which also there was pointed out, as a sufficient answer to the denunciations of it, that it related only to those who could not otherwise enter this country for any purpose except to cross to foreign territory. Any visitor possessed of the certificate of his government that he was a traveler for curiosity might, under the treaty and laws, enter and visit such an exposition, regardless of the provisions of the rule.   The same was true of a merchant, who might freely enter on a similar certificate to exhibit his goods at such an exposition.

Therefore the charges made that the provisions of this rule would exclude merchant exhibitors and bona fide visitors of China from coming to the Louisiana Purchase Exposition, and that the rule was, as a consequence, in conflict both with the laws of hospitality, since the Government had invited China, in common with other countries, to participate in said exposition, and the commercial interests of this country, were false.   The evident intent was to create by any means such a popular sentiment against this rule as would result in its modification to an extent that would render it ineffective of its purpose, that is, to prevent laborers from misusing the privilege of being admitted, for a specific purpose and fixed time, by violating the law which forbids them to reside in this country.   The misrepresentation availed to secure a single, as it was likewise a fruitless, modification by the terms of which merchant exhibitors, to whom the rule did not apply, were exempted from its provisions, and who were also, according to the terms of the modification, to be admitted upon some other evidence than the law expressly makes indispensable for such purpose.

That the suspicions of the Bureau as to the result of failure to adopt effective regulations, based upon the officially confirmed fact that, so far as known, no Chinese person ever admitted for a like purpose heretofore had left the country, were justified the following letter shows:

CONSULAR SERVICE, UNITED STATES OF AMERICA,
Hongkong, March 28.

SIR: The reports are so direct and apparently well founded that I feel it my duty to advise you that Canton has for some time past and is still certifying flocks of coolies as exhibitors to the St. Louis Fair.   I presume they are distributed between San Francisco and the northern ports.   The scheme, briefly outlined, is a cooperative association that furnishes members with articles supposed to be exhibits.   The details as to the sums paid by the villages where the coolies come from and the syndicate I can not give, but while large sums are paid in for membership, equipment, and certificates, it is provided to be repaid with interest out of the earnings of the coolie and the amount for which he sells his plant.

    *   *   *   *   *   *   *

If you can throttle and expose the rascality and rottenness and bring the perpetrators to light and justice you will have the thanks of the American in the East.

Very sincerely yours,

EDW. S. BRAGG, *Consul-General.*

Hon. F. S. STRATTON, *Collector.*

The Chinese concession at the exposition proved a financial failure. Two of the proprietors of the scheme, one a prominent Chinese "merchant" of Philadelphia, were arrested for violating the exclusion law, and the victims, who were indignant at the failure of the persons with whom they had contracted to secure their escape after landing, were deported.   The story is thus briefly told by the inspector in charge, Mr. James R. Dunn, to whose intelligence and energy, as also to the vigilance of his assistants, is due the success with which the efforts to violate the law in this manner were defeated:

OFFICE OF INSPECTOR IN CHARGE,
St. Louis, Mo., July 29, 1905.

SIR:

    *   *   *   *   *   *   *

A very large part of the work of this office during the past year dealt with the important duty of recording and maintaining surveillance of the large number of Chinese persons who were brought to the United States under special privileges accorded by law to concessionaires at the Louisiana Purchase Exposition. Of these there was a considerable number whose status was of such a character that they were released from supervision and granted every courtesy and immunity from annoying restriction. Of those over whom supervision was maintained there were 239, all of whom, with the possible exception of 4 performers, were brought within the United States for the sole purpose of evading the exclusion act by remaining in the United States unlawfully. Of said 239, 1 man escaped, but was recaptured; 1 died, 12 were arrested and deported, and the remainder, 226, returned to San Francisco by special train, under the supervision of your officers, and returned to China.

*   *   *   *   *   *   *

Respectfully,

The COMMISSIONER-GENERAL OF IMMIGRATION,
Washington, D. C.

JAMES R. DUNN,
Inspector in Charge.

Here again is doubtless another instance of the alleged harshness of administrative officers and stringency of the regulations which has contributed, since the law is now effectively enforced, to the conviction that the laws must be repealed or else that Chinese mercantile transactions in human goods, by far the most profitable merchandise from "far Cathay," will be at an end.

That is the interest at stake, for the preservation of which the bogy of the boycott has been invoked to terrify the commercial interests of the United States.

What it cost the Government approximately to protect its laws from violation by these guests at the great exposition is shown by the annexed interesting statement:

STATEMENT SHOWING DISBURSEMENTS FROM THE APPROPRIATION FOR "ENFORCEMENT OF THE CHINESE EXCLUSION ACT" INCIDENT TO THE "CHINESE VILLAGE" CONCESSION AT THE LOUISIANA PURCHASE EXPOSITION AT ST. LOUIS, MAY 1 TO NOVEMBER 30, 1904.

Transportation of 8 watchmen from San Francisco to St. Louis (guards for 184 Chinamen—arrived August 6, 1904)	$1,137.55
Transportation of 4 watchmen from San Francisco to St. Louis (guards for 53 Chinamen—arrived August 18, 1904)	414.00
Salaries of officers and employees for months of August, September, October, and November, 1904	10,853.61
Expenses of officers and employees for months of August, September, October, and November, 1904	2,142.88
Rent of offices in Chemical Building	320.00
Telephone service, Chemical Building	41.60
Towel service, Chemical Building	6.60
Ice, Chemical Building	10.40
Telephone service "Chinese Village"	67.00
Miscellaneous expenses	183.35
Transportation of 22 watchmen, St. Louis to San Francisco (guards for 232 Chinamen en route St Louis to San Francisco)	3,037.85
Total	18,214.84

This, of course, does not include the cost of arrest, trial, and deportation of those who escaped, nor of the preparing and taking of bonds at the port of entry, nor of the services of officers in identifying them at the port of departure.

RATIO OF ADMISSIONS OF CHINESE

EXEMPT FROM THE EXCLUDING PROVISION OF THE CHINESE EXCLUSION LAWS

TO DEPORTATIONS

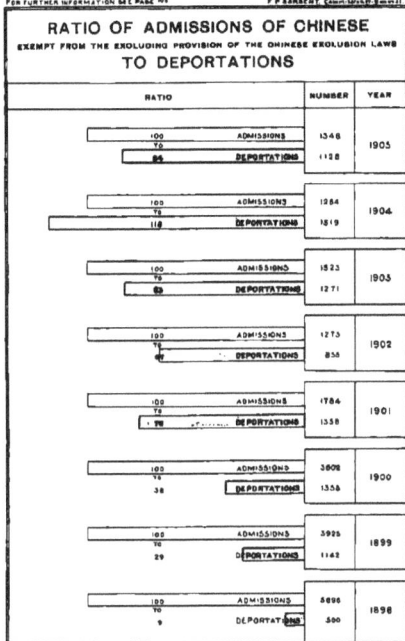

RATIO	NUMBER	YEAR
100 TO 84 — ADMISSIONS / DEPORTATIONS	1348 / 1128	1905
100 TO 118 — ADMISSIONS / DEPORTATIONS	1264 / 1819	1904
100 TO 83 — ADMISSIONS / DEPORTATIONS	1523 / 1271	1903
100 TO 67 — ADMISSIONS / DEPORTATIONS	1273 / 858	1902
100 TO 76 — ADMISSIONS / DEPORTATIONS	1784 / 1358	1901
100 TO 38 — ADMISSIONS / DEPORTATIONS	3602 / 1358	1900
100 TO 29 — ADMISSIONS / DEPORTATIONS	3925 / 1142	1899
100 TO 9 — ADMISSIONS / DEPORTATIONS	5696 / 500	1898

SAN FRANCISCO, CAL.

The subjoined table is presented to show the operation of the Chinese exclusion law during the past year at the port to which the great bulk of Chinese persons apply for admission:

REPORT OF CHINESE APPLICANTS FOR ADMISSION AT THE PORT OF SAN FRANCISCO, CAL., DURING THE FISCAL YEAR ENDING JUNE 30, 1905.

Month.	Miscellaneous.		Merchants.		Merchants' wives.		Merchants' sons.		Merchants' daughters landed.	Natives.		Under section 6.	
	Landed.	Denied.	Landed.	Denied.	Landed.	Denied.	Landed.	Denied.		Landed.	Denied.	Landed.	Denied.
1904.													
July	a 5	a 3	50	1	4	1	6	2	1	52	36	50	30
August	a 240	a 8	38	4	1	......	16	......	1	48	31	48	38
September....	......	a 11	17	2	3	......	7	3	3	26	14	42	59
October.......	a 1	a 2	27	......	1	......	10	1	......	12	10	36	19
November	......	30	22	4	5	1	1	1	2	26	8	36	22
December	1	......	29	3	......	......	4	1	......	35	4	13	13
1905.													
January	......	......	18	1	3	......	5	......	......	23	3	7	1
February	1	......	26	2	1	......	3	3	2	19	7	12	3
March	......	......	12	3	......	......	6	1	......	16	11	2	3
April	......	......	21	4	......	1	2	1	......	26	3	8	1
May	......	......	34	1	3	......	10	......	1	37	2	9	......
June..........	......	......	74	6	2	......	14	2	......	105	1	13	3
Total ...	248	54	368	31	23	3	84	15	10	425	130	276	192

Month.	Laborers with return certificates.		Natives and residents of Hawaii landed.	Landed.		Denied.		Disposition of cases.		Total cases disposed of.
	Landed.	Denied.		Male.	Female.	Male.	Female.	Landed.	Denied.	
1904.										
July	31	8	2	190	11	78	3	201	81	282
August.......	40	1	9	428	13	77	5	441	92	523
September ...	30	......	1	123	6	87	2	129	89	218
October......	42	3	4	131	2	34	1	133	35	168
November ...	30	3	2	112	12	66	3	124	69	193
December....	38	1	5	124	1	22	......	125	22	147
1905.										
January	17	2	4	73	4	10	......	77	10	87
February	15	2	1	74	6	16	1	80	17	97
March	3	1	1	36	4	19	......	40	19	59
April........	11	2	1	69	......	11	1	69	12	81
May	11	......	2	103	4	3	......	107	3	110
June	34	1	......	238	4	13	......	242	13	255
Total...	302	24	32	1,701	67	436	16	1,768	b 452	2,220

a Chinese for St. Louis Fair.   b Including 44 denied by the doctor.

Pending June 30, 1905:
- Merchants 18
- Merchants' sons 12
- Natives 48
- Under section 6 1
- Laborers with return certificates 5

Total... 84

REPORT OF CHINESE APPLICANTS FOR ADMISSION AT THE PORT OF SAN FRANCISCO, CAL., DURING THE FISCAL YEAR ENDING JUNE 30, 1905—Continued.

Month.	Seeking admission.	Departing.			Refused admission.		Arrived in transit for transfer by steamship; permitted.	Arrived in transit to depart overland; permitted.	Arrived in transit by steamship en route to China, transferred at this port.	Arrived in transit overland en route to China.	Returned by steamship company.
		Males.	Females.	Total.	Returned to China.	Deported.					
1904.											
July	246	260	15	275	32	19	140	2	26	33	
August	432	288	11	299	35	48	65		28	27	
September	88	235	3	238	39	22	27		16	20	
October	227	633	18	651	75	55	42		37	39	
November	187	630	21	651	21	61	44		49	54	
December	120	669	17	686	19	58	47		27	43	10
1905.											
January	54	225	14	239	8	6	22		14	14	3
February	94	134	4	138	11	46	64		6	18	
March	39	224	7	231	13	62	15		40	21	
April	97	107	8	115	8	9	94		40	5	
May	227	190	9	199	6	103	372		a 41	35	
June	177	128	6	134	9	20	57		20	8	
Total	1,988	3,723	133	3,856	276	509	989	2	344	317	13

a Including 1 who died at sea on the steamship City of Para.

During the fiscal year 116 cases were taken out on writs of habeas corpus, 52 of which were ordered discharged, 36 ordered remanded, and 28 are pending.

On June 30, 1904, 48 cases were pending before the Department and 266 before the Commissioner of Immigration. Total cases pending, 314.

SUMMARY.

```
Departing voluntarily ........................................................................... 3,856
Refused admission, returned to China ........................................................... 276
Deported .......................................................................................  509

    Total departing and returned to China ..................................................... 4,641
Total landed ................................................................................... 1,740

    Excess departures over admissions ........................................................ 2,901
```

The second part of this table gives first a summary for each month, showing the number applying during such month for admission, those excluded, and those deported by judicial process, as well as the number, by sex, of the voluntary departures.

It also shows the number of those coming to said port to cross by land or water to foreign territory and the number of those who have passed through any part of the United States and have departed therefrom through the port of San Francisco.

THE MEXICAN BORDER.

It is gratifying to report that, notwithstanding the natural difficulties to be surmounted, it is growing more difficult each year for Chinese persons to secure unlawful residence in this country by crossing the boundary line between the United States and Mexico at some unguarded point. This is due to the efficiency of the officers stationed along the said boundary, and to the cooperation and organization of said officers. While it is not reasonable to anticipate in the early future such perfect control as that established on the Canadian border, yet the Bureau is sanguine of establishing ultimately almost as efficient service on our southern border. One of the difficulties has been to secure such cooperation by judicial officers as will make the work of executive officers entirely successful by convincing law breakers that they can expect no immunity from success in eluding the latter at the border through the laxity of the former.   This condition is due to the situation described in the introduction to this branch of the report.

As illustrative of the difficulties presented on the Mexican border, the following extracts are given from the report of the inspector in charge at El Paso:

OFFICE CHINESE INSPECTOR IN CHARGE,
DISTRICT OF TEXAS,
El Paso, Tex., June 30, 1905.

SIR:

     *   *   *   *   *   *

From interviews with reputable American citizens residing in Mexico City, Chihuahua, Tampico, Guaymas, and other cities in the Republic of Mexico, it is learned that in the places named schools have been established, in charge of competent tutors, for the sole purpose of teaching English to the Chinese.   That the object in view of such Chinese residents of Mexico in studying English is not wholly disinterested is readily illustrated when, after having been arrested in the act of crossing the international boundary line or having been found in El Paso without certificates of residence, they blandly state in our courts, in good English, that they were born in the United States and are American citizens under a Supreme Court decision.   Inasmuch as the statements of these people are invariably corroborated by any number of Chinese witnesses, they are usually discharged by the commissioner or court and declared full-fledged American citizens, invested with the right of suffrage, and are thus placed beyond the reach of the immigration or Chinese-exclusion laws when they subsequently visit China and wish to bring back to this country their wives and children.

     *   *   *   *   *   *   *

During the past fiscal year 486 Chinese are known to have arrived in Juarez, Mexico, by Mexican Central trains, and few, if any, have returned to the interior.

As illustrating the final destination of Chinese coolies arriving in Juarez, Mexico, it may be said that when this office made an effort to inspect such arrivals, with a view to their subsequent identification when they crossed into the United States, a great many coolies were taken from the trains at a point 15 miles south of Juarez and were hauled into Juarez in wagons after night.   As to these it is not known how many arrived at the border, and they are not included in the number of known arrivals seen by inspectors.

Juarez, Mexico, across the Rio Grande from El Paso, is a town of about 7,000 people, the majority of whom are in business in El Paso.   There are now employed in Juarez the following Chinese: In laundries, 27; servants, 3; in restaurants, 11; roustabouts in dives, 5; total, 46.

     *   *   *   *   *   *   *

From 150 to 200 unemployed Chinese coolies are in the detention quarters of the smuggling firms in Juarez at all times.

The only Chinese known to have left Juarez are perhaps 200 who boarded the Sierra Madre trains for Guzman and other points near the boundary line between Mexico and Arizona, perhaps with the idea that they could probably smuggle into the United States more easily across the Arizona boundary line.

To summarize the above figures, it will be seen that during the past fiscal year 486 coolies are known to have arrived in Juarez, probably 46 coolies found employment in Juarez, practically 100 left for other border points, so that approximately 320 coolies have disappeared near the international boundary line in the vicinity of El Paso, and doubtless gained unlawful entry.

The foregoing conclusions would not seem to reflect much credit upon the energy or ability of the officers of this station in enforcing the Chinese-exclusion laws. Inviting attention to the number (49) of arrests made during the fiscal year, however, there are other important factors to be taken into consideration.   The Chinese population of El Paso, numbering about 350, is banded together as one man for the purpose of concealing and conveying into the interior of the country those Chinese coolies who have crossed the line.   A number of instances have come to light during the fiscal year where it has been discovered that some of the most influential and respected Chinese business men of El Paso have been engaged in smuggling and secreting coolies in their establishments.   Thus Chinese coolies were found secreted in the cellar of the building occupied by a prominent Chinese restaurant keeper one square from the Federal building in El Paso. * * * In certain alleys in El Paso houses occupied by Chinese have been constructed so that illegally resident Chinese can be concealed in chambers under the ground or spaces between the roof and ceiling. In fact, it is believed that the handling of Chinese coolies is the sole occupation of perhaps one-third of the Chinese population of El Paso.

Inasmuch as all passenger trains are carefully inspected when departing from El Paso, about the only feasible plan to be adopted by smugglers is to place coolies in sealed freight cars, which are shifted, through the cooperation of railroad men, so that the inspectors are unable to inspect them before their departure from El Paso. During the fiscal year two freight cars loaded with Chinese have been detected—one load of 24 at Yuma, Ariz., and one load of 19 at San Jose, Cal. It has been ascertained that the lot of 24 were placed in a Rock Island freight car near Fort Bliss, some 4 miles east of El Paso, and that the lot of 19 were placed in a freight car in New Mexico at a point some 7 miles west of El Paso. Evidence has been secured justifying the arrest of four trainmen, and the said men are now under bond for their appearance before the grand jury. In both instances the ordinary lead seals were removed and the cars were resealed under through-manifest locks, not subject to inspection by officers, by the railroad men who undertook to place the Chinamen in California.

In view of recent criticism as to the attitude of immigration officials toward members of the exempt classes, attention is called to the fact that the great majority of those claiming to be exempts are not such in fact; at least such is the case at this station. It is true that there are a number of alleged mercantile establishments whose members are ever ready to file complaints as to their ill treatment by immigration officials. With one or two exceptions, however, it can safely be said that the sole occupation of such firms in El Paso consists of selling opium to members of their own race and unfortunate Americans who have been seduced into the habit, conducting gambling establishments, and dealing in coolies at a profit of about $200 on each one placed in the United States.

Inasmuch as all Chinese persons in El Paso are engaged directly or indirectly in the smuggling of coolies, it is not seen how even those claiming to belong to the exempt classes can be allowed to secrete coolies in their establishments without subjecting themselves to "domiciliary" visits by inspectors. To hold to the contrary would be placing a premium upon smuggling and herding coolies in El Paso by every Chinese person or firm, of any class, owning or renting any kind of an establishment.

 * * * * * * *

Respectfully submitted.

T. F. SCHMUCKER,
Chinese Inspector in Charge, District of Texas.

The COMMISSIONER-GENERAL OF IMMIGRATION,
      Washington, D. C.

APPEALS IN CHINESE CASES.

The accompanying table shows the total number of cases appealed during the year from the decisions of the officers at the different ports of entry for Chinese persons, and the result of such appeals:

APPEALS OF CHINESE CASES FROM INSPECTORS' DECISIONS, FISCAL YEAR ENDED JUNE 30, 1905.

Port.	Appeals sustained.	Appeals dismissed.	Total appeals decided.
San Francisco	97	300	397
Port Townsend	7	7	14
Honolulu	2	2	4
Sumas	3	8	11
Portal		2	2
Malone	4	6	10
Total	113	325	438

While the ratio of reversals on appeal amount to about 25 per cent, much less than the ratio of reversals of boards of special inquiry in immigration appeals, still the Bureau desires in this connection to repeat the same comments made in regard to new trials of such cases. There can be no justification, as regards either the rights of Chinese applicants for admission or a just enforcement of the law, for granting new trials with the introduction of additional evidence, except in those cases where it is clearly shown that the new evidence was unattainable at the time of the original hearing, and even then the new trial should be before the original tribunal and not before the Department, whose jurisdiction, under the law as well as upon the grounds of good administration, is confined to the consideration of appeals solely upon the record on which the original decision is based.

A strict adherence to such a course will tend to diminish superfluous work both in the Department and at the ports, will hasten final decisions and avoid unnecessary delays, and will not deprive the Chinese of any reasonable opportunity to present their cases fully.

Before dismissing this subject it may be well to advert to the practice of returning cases for reinvestigation or the supply of additional evidence, not by counsel for the appellants, but by executive officers. Such returns carry with them two suggestions, both of which the Bureau believes to be detrimental to efficient administration. One is that the Department desires to reverse the officer to whom the case is returned, if it can through him secure some missing link in the chain of testimony. The other is that in some way it is the duty of the officers at the ports of entry to make a thorough search for evidence to sustain the applicant's case—a view which, if correct, would necessitate an increase in the official force at the various ports, and which is, moreover, contrary to precedent, as it is in opposition to that provision of law which requires Chinese charged with being unlawfully in this country to show affirmatively that they are entitled to reside here.

NEW CHINESE LEGISLATION.

The Bureau desires to state that it has no recommendations to make for new legislation that will make the entry of those who are entitled by treaty and the laws to come to this country more difficult. On the contrary, it believes such entry should be facilitated in every way possible, so far as may be consistent with the complete exclusion of the laboring class.

It therefore repeats, with all the urgency arising from a positive conviction of its importance, the recommendation made annually for years past. Either by law or by treaty agreement, officers of the Department, experienced in the administration of the law and accompanied by competent interpreters, should be substituted for consular and diplomatic officers of the United States in China to investigate and certify as to the claims of members of the exempt classes. Although recently there has been a marked improvement in the consular work of viséing "section 6" certificates, such work does not fall naturally within the duties of a commercial agent, who has neither sufficient time nor experience to accomplish the results which would be exacted of a trained officer of the Department. The present practice involves, moreover, a division of administrative responsibility between two distinct departments of the executive government, a condition that is cumbrous and obstructive of that unity of action and of that promptness of correction in case of fault so essential to good administration.

Such a plan would virtually substitute for the tedious investigations, under trying conditions, at the ports of entry, inquiries at the homes of the Chinese. The result, if unfavorable, would save the expense and disappointment of a long journey; and, if favorable, would save delay at the port of entry longer than would be necessary to identify the person presenting a certificate approved by a department officer in China with the person to whom it actually refers.

The Bureau is not insensible to the implication necessarily arising from this recommendation, the lack of any suspicion of which doubtless accounts for the selection of consular or diplomatic officers in China originally to perform what must have been assumed to be the rather formal indorsements of the action through its authorized representatives of the Empire of China, but, as it will show, it is dealing with an actual condition and can not stand on mere assumptions of international good faith. Such assumptions have doubtless occasioned the grievous sufferings caused by the absence of any investigations, properly so called, by the representatives of this country in China, as they have the grossly unjust charges against the officers of the Bureau.

The following statement, taken from the records of the office at San Francisco, will show the number of applicants for admission presenting "section 6" certificates, the number denied, and the number admitted for each of the last three fiscal years:

Year.	Landed.	Denied.	Total applications.
1903	186	39	225
1904	340	63	403
1905	219	154	373
Total	745	256	1,001

Thus 256, or about 25 per cent, of the total number, 1,001, of the exempt classes applying at San Francisco during the past three years, were supplied with fraudulent papers primarily by officials of their own Government. The significance of this fact as bearing upon the expediency of the foregoing recommendation, is emphasized rather than diminished by the circumstance that all these fraudulent papers were indorsed, whether perfunctorily or otherwise, by consular officers of this country in China.

The Bureau believes, moreover, that many of those admitted were not of the classes indicated by their certificates, but this belief was not susceptible of proof at the port of arrival, so remote from the residence of the applicants, and, as the law makes the mere possession of such a paper prima facie evidence of the holder's right to land, administrative officers could only admit them.

It is not possible to overestimate the practical value, both as an administrative reform and as a means of removing occasion for complaint, of the adoption of the foregoing recommendation.

For similar reasons the Bureau urges the repeal of that provision of law which requires Chinese laborers lawfully resident in the United States to conform to any other requirement than to leave their certificates of residence at the port of departure, to return to the same port, and to be identified upon such return as prerequisites to admission. The investigations of returning and departing laborers involve much labor and expense, and the results are often uncertain owing to the difficulty of securing credible evidence of the existence of the qualification upon which the right to reentry depends. The practical result is to keep many laborers in the United States who would otherwise go to China, a course that would be entirely in accord with the purpose of the treaty and laws. The limitation upon the time within which laborers must return is also open to the objection that it works much unnecessary hardship and accomplishes nothing except to prevent laborers from visiting their own country. With the repeal of these restrictions, the necessity for an interval of thirty days between the date of a Chinese laborer's application for a return certificate and the date of his departure would also cease, as would the tedious delays upon his application for readmission.

The Government having by registration agreed that laborers lawfully resident in the United States shall exercise that right, the readmission of those who have departed does not increase the number here, as probably would their untrammeled departure for absences which may become permanent. Nor does it seem necessary to penalize their departure by depriving them of the lawfully acquired right of residence, if substitutions can be prevented, as they easily can be by other and more reasonable means.

By this change one of the causes of friction and adverse criticism could be removed without weakening the laws, and at the same time a material reduction in the expense and labor of administration could be secured.

The Bureau strongly urges such a change in the Chinese exclusion law as will make it conform to the immigration laws as respects the expulsion of Chinese persons found unlawfully in the United States. For years aliens found unlawfully in this country have been arrested on executive warrant, and if, after being given an opportunity for a hearing, it appeared to the Department that they were not, under the provisions of the immigration laws, entitled to reside in our territory, they have been deported. The constitutionality of this method of expelling aliens has been affirmed by the Supreme Court in the Japanese immigrant case, and there seems to be no reason why the same plan could not be resorted to as the simplest means of expelling Chinese aliens here in violation of law. It would relieve the courts of much unnecessary labor, the enforcement of the law of many delays and some miscarriages, and would unify the operation of deporting unlawfully resident aliens, whether Chinese or of other race or origin. If such an amendment to the law can not be secured, then at least provision should be made to allow the Government the same right of appeal from the decision of a United States commissioner that is now given to the Chinese defendant.

If these three recommendations are adopted, the Bureau confidently believes that the apparent cause of complaint against the administration will be removed and leave no ground for opposition except against the policy of exclusion as applied to a solitary race or nationality. With this the Bureau has no concern, since its duty is confined to the administration of the law and has no relation to the adoption or repeal of public policies.

Reverting to the situation on the Mexican border, already described, the Bureau recommends that negotiations be opened with the Republic adjoining our southern boundary with a view to obtaining a treaty agreement, if possible, by which that Republic will agree to cooperate with the officers of this Government in preventing, as far as shall be practicable, the use of the former's territory as a basis for violations either of the immigration or Chinese-exclusion laws.

In conclusion, it is recommended that provision be made for the registration of all Chinese persons in the United States on January 1, 1900, and the issuance of new certificates of residence to those already registered. Such a law should give sufficient time for such registration, say one year from the date of its approval by the Executive, and should direct that all Chinese persons found engaged in pursuits other than those of the exempt classes after the expiration of the said period of registration be summarily deported on the warrant of the Secretary of Commerce and Labor, unless such persons can show a certificate issued to them under the new law.

The Bureau is aware that such a plan will probably legalize the residence of a number of Chinese persons not entitled under the law as it stands to reside here. . It would, however, be a lesser evil than the constant resistance to the law in behalf of those Chinese persons who in the public mind have acquired a quasi right, an equitable right, to remain because of the failure of the Government through a series of years to expel them.

While the Bureau believes that if the question could be brought before the courts their construction of existing law would put a stop to the abuse, yet it can not conclude this subject, since it has been impossible thus far to obtain a judicial hearing on any case involving ·the question, without directing attention to the remarks made in its last annual report on the violations of the exclusion law, and of the contract-labor law as well, through what it confidently believes is a misconstruction of the navigation laws, by the employment of Chinese seamen on American vessels.

There are, doubtless, circumstances under which the use of Chinese seamen is necessary to avert obstructions to our commercial intercourse with foreign countries. In such instances there can be no reasonable objection to such a course. But when vessels of American register uniformly engage Chinese seamen because they cost less or are more convenient for some actual or fancied reason, thus barring American seamen, the latter have just cause of complaint of inequality in the operation of our laws. If other classes of labor in this country are entitled to protection from unfair alien competition, seamen should be equally so; if the deck of an American vessel is, in the eye of the law, American soil to protect a Chinese person thereon during his absence from our territory, it should equally be American soil to prevent the admission thereon of Chinese not entitled to come to or reside in this country.

The subject is one that should be cleared of all doubt, uncertainty, and inconsistency by appropriate legislation, specifying the conditions ·under which Chinese seamen may be employed on American vessels in foreign ports, as also when, if at all, such seamen may be brought to this country to man such vessels.

FINANCIAL STATEMENT.

RECEIPTS AND EXPENDITURES ON ACCOUNT OF THE IMMIGRANT FUND FROM JULY 1, 1904, TO JUNE 30, 1905, AND BALANCE ON HAND JUNE 30, 1905.

Balance June 30, 1904	$1,389,403.08
Receipts fiscal year 1905	2,082,873.50
Total	3,472,276.58
Expenditures fiscal year 1905	1,508,901.13
	1,963,375.45

Act approved March 3, 1903:
For extension and addition to hospital; ferryboat; sundries, additions, repairs, and alterations to Government property; and construction of new island—amount of appropriation, $380,500; amount expended..... $43,853.07
Act approved April 28, 1904:
For widening ferry house; dredging; and construction of tugboat—amount of apprpriation $94,000; amount expended................................ 68,686.65
Act approved March 3, 1905:
For additional dredging, Ellis Island, N. Y.—amount of appropriation $100,000; amount expended... 9,791.20

Amount of special appropriations to be reimbursed from the "immigrant fund " 122,330.92

Balance June 30, 1905 .... 1,841,044.53

ITEMIZED STATEMENT OF RECEIPTS AND EXPENDITURES AT THE VARIOUS PORTS.

Port.	Receipts.	Apparent receipts.a	Expenditures.
Astoria, Oreg	$10.00		
Baltimore, Md.	127,868.00	$32.00	$34,844.36
Bangor, Me.	78.00		
Barnstable, Mass	12.00		
Beaufort, S. C	4.00		
Boston, Mass	159,531.50	1,724.44	71,521.66
Brownsville, Tex	36.00		
Brunswick, Ga	82.00		
Charleston, S. C	22.00		
Corpus Christi, Tex	1,900.00		
Eagle Pass, Tex	784.00		
El Paso, Tex	1,668.00		
Eureka, Cal.	2.00		
Fernandina, Fla.	98.00		
Galveston, Tex	5,738.00		
Gulfport, Miss	424.00		
Honolulu, Hawaii	22,694.00	154.80	18,686.45
Jacksonville, Fla	98.00		
Juneau, Alaska	28.00		
Key West, Fla	4,992.00		
Los Angeles, Cal	220.00		
Marquette, Mich	128.00		
Miscellaneous		2,317.66	536,869.18
Mobile, Ala	610.00		
Montreal, Canada	71,648.00		72,697.70
New Bedford, Mass	4,542.00		
New Orleans, La	8,332.00	2.20	13,064.05
Newport News, Va	424.00		
New York, N. Y	1,590,196.00	85,360.06	755,818.90
Nogales, Ariz	652.00		
Norfolk, Va.	470.00		
Pensacola, Fla.	568.00		
Philadelphia, Pa	49,508.00	26.50	31,356.23
Portland, Me	1,140.00		2,637.21
Portland, Oreg	518.00		
Porto Rico	3,034.00		7,460.40
Port Townsend, Wash	3,962.00		
Providence, R. I.	54.00		
Rochester, N. Y.	10.00		
San Diego, Cal	164.00		
San Francisco, Cal	14,616.00	407.00	22,060.52
Savannah, Ga	130.00		
Tampa, Fla	150.00		
Vancouver, British Columbia	5,728.00	94.05	32,003.18
	2,082,873.50	90,118.71	1,599,019.84
Less apparent receipts			90,118.71
Total	2,082,873.50		1,508,901.13

a Apparent receipts represent amounts recovered on account of overpayments, disallowances made by the Auditor, and repayments to the appropriation from various sources.

Appropriation for the enforcement of the Chinese-exclusion act, 1905 .... $600,000.00
Disbursements on account of salaries and traveling expenses of inspectors, together with amount expended in the deportation of Chinese here in violation of law............... 533,223.11

From the foregoing statement it will be seen that the net balance on hand, after payment of all expenses incident to the administration of the laws and regulations in regard to immigration, and of the sum of $122,330.92 for improvements and alterations, ferryboat, new island, dredging, etc., at Ellis Island Immigrant Station, is $1,841,044.53. This is an increase over the balance on hand at the corresponding period last year of $451,641.45. The total expenditures for the execution of the immigration laws were, at the various points named in the above table, $1,508,901.13. This total of course is exclusive of the payment from the "immigrant fund" (head-tax receipts) of $122,330.92 for repairs, etc., at Ellis Island, above referred to.

CHINESE DEPORTATION

In the Northeastern States 55
In the Northwestern States 112
Other parts of the United States 454

Total 621

As will be seen from the accompanying financial statement, the total cost of making deportations was $67,730.61, an average cost of $109.07 for each Chinese deported.

Expended for salaries and expenses of officers and miscellaneous items. $465,492.50
Expended for deportation of prisoners entering the United States from the Canadian border 19,629.27
Expended for deportation of prisoners entering the United States at other points 48,101.34

NOTE.—Seventy-three Chinese have been deported, at an expense of $8,951.18, who are not included in the above statement, the expense of their deportation having been paid, during the fiscal year 1905, from the appropriation for the fiscal year 1904.

CHARTS.

Accompanying the report the Bureau presents charts which contain in graphic form information in regard to immigration, admissions and deportations of Chinese, and results obtained by an investigation of the penal, reformatory and charitable institutions of the United States.

CHART 1 (following page 6).—IMMIGRANTS DEBARRED AND RETURNED.

This chart shows the proportion of aliens refused admission, and the proportion of those admitted that afterwards became public charges and were returned under the provisions of the immigration laws to the countries whence they came. It is interesting to note the balance between the debarred and the returned, as shown by the uniformity of divergence and convergence of the wave lines representing these two classes.

During the fourteen years shown about 60,000 aliens have been debarred, of which number 67 per cent were paupers or aliens likely to become public charges, 17 per cent were contract laborers, and 13 per cent were aliens suffering from loathsome or dangerous contagious diseases.

Although each year several hundred aliens have been returned to the countries whence they came because they were public charges, and several thousand others were originally refused admission to the United States because likely to become public charges, in the investigation of the charitable institutions of the country conducted by this Bureau in 1904 about 30,000 alien paupers, including insane, were also found in the public institutions, and another 5,000 in the charitable institutions under private control. In addition thereto there were about 10,000 alien criminals found in the penal institutions, making a total, in round numbers, of 45,000, of whom 40,000 are supported exclusively at public expense. There are also over 57,000 naturalized foreigners in these institutions. (See Chart 5.)

CHART 2 (following page 10).—ALIEN CONTRACT LABORERS.

The following three phases with reference to alien contract laborers debarred since 1892 are presented by this chart, viz:
1. Number of contract laborers debarred each year.
2. Contract laborers compared with total immigration.
3. Contract laborers compared with aliens debarred from all causes.

It will be seen that during each of the last three years a greater number of contract laborers was debarred than during any previous year; during each of the first five years a greater proportion of aliens debarred from all causes was contract laborers than during any subsequent year, while the ratio of contract laborers to total immigration averaged highest during the intermediate period 1894–1900.

RACE CLASSIFICATION.

Ninety-five per cent of the immigration to this country comes from Europe. This European immigration may be separated by race into well-recognized divisions, which conform more or less to geographical location. With the assistance of Prof. Otis T. Mason, curator of ethnology, National Museum, most of these different races or peoples, or more properly subdivisions of race, coming from Europe have been grouped into four grand divisions, as follows:

Teutonic division, from northern Europe: German, Scandinavian, English, Dutch, Flemish, and Finnish.

Iberic division, from southern Europe: South Italian, Greek, Portuguese, and Spanish; also Syrian from Turkey in Asia.

Keltic division, from western Europe: Irish, Welsh, Scotch, French, and North Italian.

Slavic division, from eastern Europe: Bohemian, Moravian, Bulgarian, Servian, Montenegrin, Croatian, Slovenian, Dalmatian, Bosnian, Herzegovinian, Hebrew, Lithuanian, Polish, Roumanian, Russian, Ruthenian, and Slovak.

The Mongolic division has also been added, to include Chinese, Japanese, Korean, East Indian, Pacific Islander, and Filipino.

Under "all others" have been included Magyar, Turkish, Armenian, African (black), and subdivisions native to the Western Hemisphere.

By reason of blood mixture this classification is somewhat arbitrary, especially with regard to Finnish, Scotch, and southern Germans.

CHART 3 (following page 16).—RACES OF IMMIGRANTS.

This chart shows approximately areas of racial grand divisions of Europe, together with number and ethnic character of aliens arriving from each European country. A comparison of the number of aliens of the different racial subdivisions and grand divisions for the fiscal year 1905 is also shown.

With regard to grand division of race, during the past year 37 per cent of the entire immigration, or 384,679 aliens, were Slavic; 21 per cent, or 213,801, were Iberic; 22 per cent, or 221,019, were Teutonic; and 12 per cent, or 124,218, were Keltic. There was an increase in the proportion of Slavic from 33½ per cent in 1904 to 37½ per cent in 1905, while the Teutonic and Iberic decreased from 24 and 23 per cent, respectively, in 1904, to 22 and 21 per cent in 1905. The Keltic remained the same.

CHART 4 (following page 34).—PROPORTION OF IMMIGRATION TO EACH STATE.

This chart is designed to show graphically the proportion of immigration to the different States and sections of the country for the fiscal year 1904. The enormous proportion going to New York, Pennsylvania, and the North Atlantic section shows prominently.

The North Atlantic and North Central States this year received 90 per cent of the entire immigration, compared with 89 per cent the previous year, the North Atlantic States getting 68 per cent and the North Central States 22 per cent, compared with 67 and 22 per cent, respectively, during the previous year. The entire South received but 4 per cent of the total immigration, 3 per cent going to the South Atlantic States and 1 per cent to the South Central States. The proportions for this section were the same as those of last year. The Western States received but 4 per cent during 1905, which is a decrease from 6 per cent in 1904. (See text for Chart 9 under head of "General distribution.")

CHART 5 (following page 62).—INMATES OF PENAL, REFORMATORY, AND CHARITABLE INSTITUTIONS—EXCEPT PRIVATE CHARITABLE.

This chart shows all inmates of the above institutions, divided into aliens, naturalized foreign born, and native born. Information with regard to aliens only was collected by the Bureau of Immigration, and is more fully shown by States in Chart 8, and by races in tables on page —. The said chart and tables, however, include 5,339 alien inmates of private charitable institutions, which were omitted from this chart (No. 5) for lack of information as to native born and naturalized foreign born. Data with regard to the latter two classes were collected by the Bureau of the Census and furnished in advance of the regular compilation, and are therefore subject to slight change, which, however, will not affect the general proportions.

It is shown by this chart that there are 349,885 inmates of these institutions, 252,811 of whom are native born and 97,074 foreign born. Of the foreign born, 39,646 are still aliens, and 57,428 have become naturalized. Thus, 11 per cent of the total number of inmates of these institutions are aliens, and 17 per cent are naturalized foreign born, making a total foreign born within the institutions of 28 per cent, although of the total population of the United States but 14 per cent were foreign born, according to the last census.

CHART 6 (following page 84).—CHINESE BY CLASSES.

The left side of this chart shows disposition of cases of Chinese applying for admission, except citizens of the United States. The right side shows disposition of those arrested within the United States because here in violation of the Chinese exclusion laws.

On the left the class of admissions, under the head of "Exempt," represents all alien Chinese allowed to enter the United States, except those shown in chart under the titles of "Transit" and "Returning laborers." The former pass through and out of the United States, and the latter are those Chinese who resided here at the time of the passage of the Chinese exclusion act, were properly registered at that time, and are now returning to the United States after a temporary absence. The "Exempt," therefore, represent the Chinese admissions proper, with regard to which it is interesting to note the gradual decrease in the number each year. This decrease of admissions compared with deportations is made the subject of Chart 7.

Chinese applicants of all classes who were refused admission to the United States are shown under the title "Denied."

It will be noticed, on the right, that the number of arrests of Chinese within the United States, because here in violation of law, has gradually increased from 566 in 1899 to 1,793 in 1904, although during the past year (1905) the number of arrests dropped back to 1,088.

The following information, which does not show in chart, is of special interest: During the past fiscal year the total number of Chinese allowed to enter the United States (exclusive of those in transit) was 2,605, of whom 634 were citizens of the United States and 1,971 were aliens. Again, of the 2,605 total, 1,805 had resided here before, and 800 were new arrivals. Of the same total, 1,838, or 71 per cent, arrived at San Francisco; and of the 481 total denied, 364, or 76 per cent, arrived at that port.

CHART 7 (following page 92).—RATIO OF ADMISSIONS OF CHINESE TO DEPORTATIONS.

All Chinese deported to China because attempting to enter the United States unlawfully or because unlawfully residing here are shown in Chart 6 under the heads "Denied admission to United States and deported to China" and "Convicted and deported to China." The sum of these two classes therefore represents all Chinese sent back to China by United States authorities. As explained in text for Chart 6, "Exempt" represent Chinese admissions proper.

A comparison of the admissions as above with the deportations since 1898 shows a progressive efficiency in the administration of the Chinese-exclusion laws, as follows: In 1898 there were 9 deportations to every 100 admissions; in 1899 the ratio increased to 29 to 100; in 1900 it was 36 to 100; in 1901, 76 to 100; in 1902, 67 to 100; in 1903, 83 to 100, and in the year 1904 the number of deportations was actually larger than the admissions, being in the ratio of 118 deportations to 100 admissions. During the past year the admissions were 1,348, and deportations 1,128, the ratio being 100 admissions to 84 deportations.

CHART 8.—ALIENS DETAINED IN PENAL, REFORMATORY, AND CHARITABLE INSTITUTIONS OF EACH STATE.

This chart gives the following information with reference to alien inmates of penal, reformatory, and charitable institutions of each State: Sex; whether under or over 21 years of age; probable period of detention; length of time in the United States, and whether confined in penal, insane, or other charitable institutions; whether said institutions are under private, county and municipal, State, or Federal jurisdiction; and in the case of criminals, whether offenses are grave or minor. Thus a brief record of each State is shown, from which the approximate cost of maintenance of aliens in any State can be estimated,.and the conditions in any State can be readily compared with those in another.

Attention is invited to the fact that the States in which are located the large cities have the largest proportions of aliens detained in their institutions. For instance, out of 44,985 aliens in all the institutions of the United States, 12,440, or 28 per cent, are in the State of New York; 5,601, or 12½ per cent, in Pennsylvania; 5,490, or 12 per cent, in Massachusetts; and 3,359, or 7½ per cent, in Illinois, making a total of 26,890 in the four States mentioned, which is 60 per cent of the entire number in the United States.

It was found impracticable to separate reformatory from other penal institutions. Therefore both have been included under the head of "penal." Juvenile delinquents have been here included, the number of which is approximately represented by the number of aliens in penal institutions under 21 years of age.

Institutions for criminal insane are placed with penal institutions. Inmates of all other asylums for the insane are placed under the head of institutions for the insane.

Inmates of almshouses, juvenile asylums, homes, institutions for the feeble-minded, and other charitable institutions (except institutions for the insane) are placed under the head of charitable institutions.

With regard to inmates of penal institutions the period of "probable detention" is definite; with regard to inmates of charitable institutions and institutions for the insane the period of probable detention is approximate.

· Crimes have been divided into two classes, viz, grave and minor. Under the head of grave crimes have been included murders, robberies, burglaries, and other offenses usually enumerated with the serious crimes. The misdemeanors or lesser offenses, including incorrigibility, are classed under the head of "minor" offenses.

Information as to the length of time in the United States was not obtainable from all aliens. Percentages under the head of "Years in the United States" therefore represent averages based upon answers of aliens from whom this information could be obtained.

With regard to the length of time these aliens have been in the United States, 34 per cent have been here less than ten years and 62 per cent have been here less than twenty years.

With regard to sex, age, and cause of detention, 65 per cent are males and 35 per cent females; 88 per cent are 21 years of age and over and 12 per cent under 21; 22 per cent were detained for crime, 45 per cent because of insanity, and 33 per cent for pauperism. There is a great variation between the different racial divisions with regard to sex, age, and causes of detention. (See Race classification, p. 103, and Table 1, p. 60.)

The Teutonic element in these institutions is composed largely of German, English, and Scandinavian; the Keltic largely of Irish and Scotch; the Iberic of Italian, and the Slavic of Polish, Hebrew, and other racial subdivisions from Russia and Austria-Hungary.

With regard to sex, 4 per cent of the Mongolic, 15 per cent of the Iberic, 30 and 32 per cent, respectively, of the Slavic and Teutonic, and 50 per cent of the Keltic divisions are females.

As to age, the Teutonic, Keltic, and Mongolic have each not more than 8 per cent under 21, while the Iberic and Slavic have, respectively, 26 and 27 per cent under that age.

As to causes of detention, of those detained for crime, the Iberic leads, 39 per cent of all alien inmates of the Iberic grand division being detained for that cause, the proportion of Slavic being 25 per cent, of Teutonic 17 per cent, and Keltic 15 per cent.   As a matter of interest in this connection, it may be stated that there were 809 aliens confined in the institutions of the United States for murder, 253 of whom were Italians; there were 373 confined for attempts to kill, 139 of whom were Italians.   This is a ratio of 1 Italian to 2 aliens of all other races, while the proportion of inmates in all the institutions is 1 Italian to 13 aliens of all other races.

With regard to those detained for insanity, the order is practically reversed, being 55 per cent of the Teutonic, 49 per cent of the Keltic, 34 per cent of the Slavic, and 24 per cent of the Iberic.

With regard to those detained for pauperism, the proportions are 41 per cent of the Slavic, 37 per cent of the Iberic, 36 per cent of the Keltic, and 28 per cent of the Teutonic.

Thus it is seen that the Iberic races have a greater predisposition to crime, the Slavic to pauperism, and the Teutonic and Keltic to insanity.

But 2 per cent of all the inmates of the various institutions were Mongolic, a very large number of whom were Chinese detained awaiting trial upon the charge of being in the United States in violation of the Chinese-exclusion laws.   With regard to cause of detention, therefore, the Mongolic can not be properly compared with the other racial divisions and have been omitted from the foregoing comparison.

CHART 9.—RACES, OCCUPATIONS, AND INCREASE AND DECREASE OF IMMIGRATION, BY STATES (DESTINATION).

GENERAL DISTRIBUTION.

Diagrams shown on this map, indicating the yearly increase and decrease in each State's proportion of the entire immigration to the United States, show progressively increasing proportions of immigrants going to the group of States consisting of Pennsylvania, Ohio, and West Virginia, while the percentage for the State of New York has gradually decreased from 42 per cent in 1892 to 30 per cent in 1905.

It is noticeable that until recently the far Western States had been attracting increasing proportions of the country's immigration, and the Middle West and South decreasing percentages year by year. This fact shows prominently in Chart 3 in annual report for the fiscal year 1903.   This condition is now distinctly changed.   Most of the Eastern States, aside from some of those in which are located the principal ports of entry, show increases.   This wave of increase runs westward through Pennsylvania, West Virginia, Ohio, Indiana, Illinois, and Missouri, while north and south of those States, with two or three exceptions, decreases are general.   Thus the Western States now receive smaller proportions of the country's immigration.

In some respects, however, aliens are better distributed now than formerly, as shown by the fact that smaller proportions are now remaining in the States in which are located the principal ports of entry, thereby in a small degree tending to check the increasing congestion of aliens in those States and the large cities located therein. In fact, but three States in which large cities are located, viz, Pennsylvania, Ohio, and Missouri, show increases. With regard to that portion of the United States south of Mason and Dixon's line, the only State showing an increase, aside from distinctly Eastern States, is Mississippi.

RACIAL DISTRIBUTION.

Iberic and Slavic divisions: Seventy-five per cent of the immigration going to the group of seven States, New York, Pennsylvania, New Jersey, Ohio, Delaware, Maryland, and West Virginia, which group receives 62 per cent of the entire immigration to the United States, belong to the Iberic races of southern Europe (principally South Italian) and Slavic races of eastern Europe, including Magyars from Hungary. Of the great bulk of immigration going to New York, 32 per cent is South Italian and 24 per cent Hebrew. Other Eastern and Southern States, and Indiana, Illinois, and Missouri get large percentages of immigrants belonging to the Iberic and Slavic divisions. Louisiana is conspicuous because of heavy percentage of South Italian.

Teutonic division: The North Central and Northwestern States get heavy percentages of immigrants of Teutonic blood from northern Europe, the States of Michigan, Minnesota, North and South Dakota, Iowa, Kansas, Nebraska, and Utah, each receiving from 59 to 90 per cent of immigrants of this class.

Keltic division: New England and some of the Southern States show moderate proportions of immigrants of the Keltic division. This class of immigrants, however, is most conspicuously represented in the Southwest and Rocky Mountain regions.

Mongolic division: Most of the immigrants of the Mongolic division, principally Japanese, go to Hawaii and the Pacific coast. Of all the immigrants going to Hawaii, 75 per cent are Japanese.

OCCUPATIONS.

Character of the immigration to certain States and sections with regard to occupation is conspicuously shown by the variation in the proportions of the two great classes designated under the heads of "laborers" and "no occupation." (Immigrants classed under the head of "no occupation" are composed almost entirely of women and children. This class therefore largely represents families.)

An examination of the chart shows that immigration to the mining regions of the Alleghenies, Lake Superior, and Rocky Mountains is composed of comparatively few families and a very large proportion of laborers, while that to the agricultural districts of the Middle West and South is composed of comparatively few laborers and large proportions of families. The latter fact is conspicuously the case with regard to the tier of seven prairie States and Territories from North Dakota to Texas, where nearly half the immigration consists of women and children classed under the head "no occupation," with a corresponding decrease in the proportion of laborers. It is notable also that the Teutonic element in the immigration to this tier of States predominates, as it also does in the immigration to the States forming our northwestern boundary and those adjacent thereto.

CHART 10.—CHANGES IN SOURCES OF IMMIGRATION WHICH HAVE
CAUSED HEAVY INCREASE OF ILLITERACY.

By this chart illiteracy of immigrants from the different countries
during the past six years is compared with a like period twenty years
ago.   The earlier period of the comparison was selected as representing the period of heaviest immigration previous to the present influx.
The change from northern and western Europe to southern and eastern
Europe had then just commenced.   Illiteracy statistics were not then
being collected.   Illiteracy shown for the earlier period is based upon
the assumption that the rate of illiteracy for the various countries then
was practically the same as now.   The point illustrated is that the
change in the source of immigration from the Teutonic and Keltic
countries of northern and western Europe to the Iberic and Slavic
countries of southern and eastern Europe has greatly increased the
quantity of illiterates annually arriving, who are represented in chart
by the red centers.

CHART 11.—ILLITERACY BY RACE.

This chart shows graphically the increase and decrease of arrivals
from the different countries and of the various racial divisions since
1899; also the percentage of illiterates of each race for 1904.

There has been an increase in the average illiteracy of all aliens
admitted from 25 per cent in 1904 to 26 per cent in 1905.   The principal races contributing to this increase are, of the Slavic division,
Polish, Croatian, Lithuanian, and Ruthenian, which increased, respectively, from 36, 36, 54, and 59 per cent in 1904, to 40, 38, 57, and 63
per cent in 1905; of the Iberic, the Italian (south) increased from 54 to
56 per cent.   The Italian (north) also increased from 13 to 14 per cent.

Some of the races show decreases, the most important of which are
Slovak from 28 to 25 per cent, Greek from 24 to 23 per cent, and
Finnish from 3 to 2 per cent.

CHART 12.—IMMIGRATION BY COUNTRIES.

This chart shows the yearly immigration from the principal countries from 1820 to the present year.   The proportions from each country during the entire period are as follows: United Kingdom, 33 per
cent; Germany, 23 per cent; Scandinavia (Denmark, Norway, and
Sweden), 8 per cent; Italy, 8 per cent; Austria-Hungary, 8 per cent;
Russia, 6 per cent; France, 2 per cent; Switzerland, 1 per cent; countries not specified, 11 per cent.

It is estimated that about 46 per cent of our population is due to
immigration since colonial times.   The nationalities shown in chart
would, therefore, practically represent the origins of 46 per cent of
the population.   It will be seen by reference to chart, however, that
until very recent times immigration was almost entirely from the Teutonic and Keltic countries of northern and western Europe, principally
Germany and the United Kingdom.   Previous to 1820, although no
immigration statistics were collected, it is known that the people who
came to this country during colonial times and after were also from
northern and western Europe.   Thus the great mass of our population
is of Teutonic and Keltic origin, with a considerably greater propor-

tion of the former. These people brought with them the character and thrift of northwestern Europe. This fact is undoubtedly responsible in a very large degree for the position this country has taken among the foremost nations of the world. A change in the source of immigration it will be seen, however, commenced about 1882 and has assumed enormous proportions during the past eight years, until now 70 per cent of our immigration comes from the Slavic and Iberic countries of southern and eastern Europe, 700,000 having arrived from those countries during the past year, among whom were great numbers of illiterate aliens of different race, customs, and standards.

Starting eight years ago, the time when this change commenced to assume such great proportions, and computing the immigration and natural increase thereon, it will be found that the increase to our population from this source, if immigration and natural increase continue at the present rate, will more than keep pace with the natural increase in the population here at that time; 1.466 per cent, the annual rate of natural increase during the past decade, is used in this calculation. Thus, with the continuance of present conditions, it will be seen, the time will come when the new element, containing 70 per cent from southeastern Europe, will outnumber the old, which eventually can hardly mean less than a changed nationality.

CHART 13.—WAVE OF IMMIGRATION TO THE UNITED STATES SINCE 1820.

This chart shows the wave of immigration into the United States from the various countries since 1820. It is interesting to note the successive periodical increases, receding less each time, coincident with periods of financial depression, only to reach a greater height with the next ascending wave and passing the million mark, the highest point in history, during the past year. Thus the three periods of depression following 1857, 1873, and 1893 stand out prominently. This periodical rise and fall well represent the relative prosperity of the country, while the gradual average increase from decade to decade may be taken as an index of the country's development and growth and its capacity to employ larger quantities of the alien element.

What will be the effect if the present phenomenal immigration continues is a question that is constantly being asked. With regard more particularly to quantity the question may be answered by the following illustration: China proper is the thickly populated portion of the Chinese Empire and is the country popularly thought of as practically representing the limit of density of population. At the present rate of immigration, say 1,000,000 per annum, and the present rate of natural increase (14.66 per cent per decade), the United States would reach the density of China proper in about four generations, or, more particularly, in one hundred and thirty-six years, at which time we would have a population of 950,000,000. This is in no sense an estimate of future population; it is simply an answer to the mathematical problem as to how long it will take to reach a density of population equal to the estimated density of China proper, with an annual immigration of 1,000,000, at the present rate of natural increase, and represents the present pace.

GENERAL.

It would be unjust to close this report, which the Bureau has endeavored to abbreviate as much as consistent with the importance of the subjects to be treated, without commenting on the intelligence, industry, and fidelity of its officers. They are spread throughout the country from Maine to southern California. Some are stationed in Honolulu, some in Porto Rico, and many of them in Canada. They number some 1,214, thoroughly organized under competent chiefs, many of them working regardless of hours, whether breaking the seals of freight cars on the southern border to prevent the smuggling of Chinese or watching the countless routes of ingress from Canada, ever alert and willing, equally efficient in detecting the inadmissible alien and the pretended citizen. The Bureau asserts with confidence that, excepting a very few, the Government of this country has no more able and faithful servants in its employ, either civil or military, than the immigration officers.

Only the rules necessarily adopted to prevent the reports of the bureaus and departments from assuming undue length and elaboration have restrained the Bureau from reproducing at length some of the many valuable reports from its commissioners and officers in charge. All of them contain valuable information, of great practical use to the people of this country, but it has been possible to reproduce herein only a part of some of them, and, in some instances, to adopt the valuable suggestions made in them.

Notwithstanding the length to which it has extended, I do not feel, in presenting the report of its operations during the third year of my administration, that the work of the Bureau has been fully reported; neither do I feel that it could properly have been further abbreviated. The subject of immigration is the most far-reaching in importance of all those with which this Government has to deal. The history of the world offers no precedent for our guidance, since no such peaceful invasion of alien peoples has ever before occurred. It must have great and largely unforeseen effects upon our form of civilization, our social and political institutions, and, above all, upon the physical, mental, and moral characteristics of our people.

Can such a subject be considered too seriously or too minutely? I can not think it possible. The danger lies in the opposite direction.

Respectfully,

F. P. SARGENT,
Commissioner-General.

The SECRETARY OF COMMERCE AND LABOR.

.

INDEX.

INDEX OF CHARTS.

INDEX OF TABLES.

O

www.ingramcontent.com/pod-product-compliance
Lightning Source LLC
Chambersburg PA
CBHW031439280326
41927CB00038B/1146